UNCIVIL WARS

UNCIVIL WARS

International Security and the New Internal Conflicts

Donald M. Snow

BOULDER
LONDON

Published in the United States of America in 1996 by
Lynne Rienner Publishers, Inc.
1800 30th Street, Boulder, Colorado 80301

and in the United Kingdom by
Lynne Rienner Publishers, Inc.
3 Henrietta Street, Covent Garden, London WC2E 8LU

Library of Congress Cataloging-in-Publication Data
Snow, Donald M., 1943–
UnCivil wars : international security and the new internal conflicts / Donald M. Snow.
p. cm.
Includes bibliographical references and index.
ISBN 1-55587-648-X (alk. paper).
ISBN 1-55587-655-2 (pbk. : alk. paper)
1. National security. 2. Security, International. 3. Civil war. I. Title.
UA10.5.S62 1996
327.1'7—dc20 96-8158
CIP

British Cataloguing in Publication Data
A Cataloguing in Publication record for this book
is available from the British Library.

Printed and bound in the United States of America

The paper used in this publication meets the requirements of the American National Standard for Permanence of Paper for Printed Library Materials Z39.48-1984.

5 4 3 2 1

Contents

Tables and Figures

TABLES

FIGURES

Preface

This manuscript was inspired, if that is the right word, by my observation of the series of post–Cold War internal wars in such places as Bosnia and Herzegovina, Somalia, Rwanda, and Haiti. Each of these conflicts, and others I subsequently investigated, seemed to be conducted differently from more conventional insurgencies we had studied during the Cold War. These later conflicts were curiously nonmilitary: In places like Bosnia, Somalia, Liberia, and Rwanda, the armed forces never seemed to fight one another; instead, what passed for "military action" was the more or less systematic murder and terrorizing of civilian populations. The armed forces displayed a brutality of conduct for which the only Cold War parallel I can draw is the Khmer Rouge rampage in Cambodia during the 1970s.

My sense of contrast derives from a book I published in 1993 called *Distant Thunder: Third World Conflict and the New International Order.* That book started from the premise that most internal wars were guerrilla wars fought over political ideologies and the gaining of control over the government, and that most employed some form of Maoist mobile-guerrilla strategy. Those wars, I argued, intensely intermix political and military action in the crucial battle for the hearts and minds of men. The effect is to simultaneously make these conflicts sophisticated and, more important, to moderate the violence that occurs in them.

The new wars are clearly not like that. There is no common center of gravity to which the combatants appeal; in many cases it is not clear that the "insurgents" have any interest in or intent on gaining political power or responsibility; and there is little sense of boundaries on the extent of violence both sides would commit. These conflicts seem, indeed, to be a new breed of internal war.

If that is true, I reason, it has important implications for international politics and military affairs. These wars are almost the whole of the fabric of violent conflict in the post–Cold War era. They do not threaten to rend the fabric of international politics, and the fact that, occurring as they do on the peripheries of the international system, they are the biggest problem of war we face is an indication that the world is a less threatening place than it was during the Cold War.

There is, however, the practical problem that these conflicts exist and thanks to global television they are very public, and sometimes the international system (including the United States) will be tempted to try to intervene and staunch the slaughter. My sense is that we are not well organized to understand and deal with these kinds of conflict because the framework with which we approach them is that of the Cold War: traditional wars of national liberation. Our understanding is of insurgency, counterinsurgency, and the dynamics of intervention in insurgency situations.

That framework may be inadequate, even irrelevant, to understanding and responding to the new internal wars. When I began to think about and to write this book, I was mostly concerned with the international systemic impact; and much of that emphasis remains. The more I thought about the problem, however, the more apparent became the central role of the United States in systemic responses. Thus, somewhat subtly, the added consideration of what U.S. policy should be began to creep into the formula. With the formation of the Implementation Force in December 1995 for dispatch to Bosnia, that change in emphasis seemed redeemed.

These concerns motivated the pages that follow. The first chapter explores how the international system has changed since the end of the Cold War and introduces the idea of new internal war. The second chapter looks at underlying causes of internal war and explores particularly how they have changed. Chapter 3 examines the traditional models of insurgency-counterinsurgency and how they may or may not apply to the new wars. Chapter 4 describes the new internal wars in terms of distinctive characteristics. Chapter 5 looks at possible forms of systemic response, sounding a generally discouraging, cautionary note. The final chapter examines the likely future constellation of these conflicts.

—Donald M. Snow

UNCIVIL WARS

1

Violence in the Post–Cold War System

One of the most dramatic ways in which the post–Cold War world differs from the Cold War international system is in the pattern of violence that has been developing. Warfare in its most traditional sense has virtually disappeared from the scene. There has not been a major (or for that matter, minor) cross-border war between states since Iraq's invasion of Kuwait in 1990 and the counterinvasion by the American-led coalition in February 1991, unless one counts those actions taken by the Croatian army to recapture Serb-held Croatian territory (what the Serbs called Krajina) in August 1995, and border fighting between Peru and Ecuador. (Arguably, the post–Cold War world is currently too young to know if this situation is significant or anomolous.) A different, in many ways darker, pattern of violence has begun to emerge. Its prototypes include well-publicized outbreaks of violence in places such as Somalia and Ethiopia, and the less well-documented cases of Sierre Leone, Liberia, Georgia, Tajikistan, and Sri Lanka.

These wars (and often the use of that term glorifies what is going on) are all internal: fought primarily between groups within countries rather than between states. Civil wars have of course been going on between groups within political units for as long as states or their equivalents have existed. But these internal wars are somehow different from the wars we have traditionally thought of as civil conflicts: They seem, for instance, less principled in political terms, less focused on the attainment of some political ideal. They seem more vicious and uncontrolled in their conduct; one cannot find the restraining influence of Maoist or other political philosophies. Instead, these wars often appear to be little more than rampages by groups within states against one another with little or no apparent ennobling purpose or outcome; they are, indeed, uncivil wars.

There is a small but growing literature that is beginning to look at aspects of this new form of violence. Pathfinding works like Daniel Patrick Moynihan's *Pandaemonium* and William Pfaff's *The Wrath of Nations* have examined the phenomenon of nationalism and found it to be part of the explanation of the new pattern. The practice of "ethnic cleansing" in Bosnia has added ethnicity (see Ted Robert Gurr's *Ethnic Conflict in World Affairs,* for instance), and others have chosen to look at the corrosive effects on the international system of nationalistically based and justified violence (Gidon Gotlieb's *Nation Against State* is an example). Each of these forces provides an explanation, a motivation, or even an excuse for violence; no one of them by itself, however, can account for the entirety of the phenomenon.

One result of this new literature has been to raise questions about how, if at all, the international system should deal with this spate of violence. Most of these wars occur in what are, from an American perspective, very remote places (as I will argue, especially in Africa, central, and south Asia), but the unrelenting eye of global television makes them more difficult to ignore than was the case in an earlier period. When, for instance, widespread slaughter occurred in Rwanda in the early 1960s, hardly anyone in the West outside the community of experts noticed; when it reoccurred in 1994, it filled the nightly news on television, the front pages of newspapers, and the covers of major news magazines. The conflict was virtually impossible for even the casual observer to ignore. It remains to be seen whether we will see so much of this carnage that we will become desensitized to it.

Our initial reaction, activated and then doused in Somalia, was to try to intervene. Leading the charge, especially in 1992, was a newly aggressive United Nations and its Secretary-General, Boutros Boutros-Ghali, who proclaimed in *An Agenda for Peace* a broad mandate that would "empower" the world body as the agency of choice for dealing with this new phenomenon. That enthusiasm waned as the true underlying political problems of Somalia proved more intractable than the politically motivated starvation the effort originally addressed. The UN has come to suffer from a lack of adequate resources, human and financial, and lacking the intellectual framework, and the political will to act, it cannot act as the savior of a system faced with a new structure of problems. But no one else has volunteered to fill the role.

The question of what, if anything, the system should do is becoming more important because the new internal war, as I will refer to it, is *the* major form that violence and instability are now taking. As the Cold War's residues (the end of communism, for instance) have receded, there is very little familiar to us, in a national-security sense. The threat of war among the major powers of the world is virtually nonexistent, and even the "threat" of regional conflicts or of nuclear or other proliferators seems remote. The very fact that we can now spend considerable effort on such concerns—which were peripheral matters during the Cold War—shows how much the situation has changed. If one is going to prepare for the real opportunities to employ military forces in the world, the new internal wars must be at or near the top of the agenda for which those preparations are made.

If my description is accurate, the resulting situation is perplexing: If new internal war in remote parts of the world is indeed the principal form of contemporary systemic violence, the world is a more stable place—very few of these wars, for instance, affect the major powers greatly. At the same time, these problems and their solutions are likely to be more intractable than during the Cold War. Violence in the system, in other words, is simultaneously less important and more difficult to manage than it was before.

The new internal wars are a sufficiently different phenomenon to warrant intellectual and policy attention. They have broken out in the context of a greatly changed international environment, and an analysis must therefore begin by describing and assessing that environment. One of the characteristics of that new environment has been the emergence of very poor, very unstable states—the so-called failed states—that seem to be the locus of a disproportionate amount of the violence that afflicts the system.

After examining, in Chapters 1 and 2, the traditional, Cold War–based view of the political and economic circumstances in which internal wars occurred, and looking at the current situation, we turn in Chapters 3 and 4 to the nature and structure of the new wars, beginning with a comparative emphasis on classic patterns of insurgency and counterinsurgency and how these new wars vary from that pattern. This analysis will provide in Chapter 5 some instruction on what kinds of outside response is possible and not possible. Finally, in Chapter 6 we turn our attention to the likely pattern in the future.

DIMENSIONS OF CHANGE IN THE INTERNATIONAL ORDER

The world has changed markedly since the largely unanticipated demise of the Cold War and the even more widely unanticipated implosion of the chief antagonist of the Cold War era, the Soviet Union. The result has been a major change in the operation of the international system on the order of magnitude of the end of the world wars. As I have argued elsewhere (notably in *The Shape of the Future,* second edition), what distinguishes the transition from the Cold War system to the post–Cold War system is that the planning for the post–World War II world that occurred during that war simply did not occur. The reason, of course, is that so few anticipated the change. Thus, the process of adaptation that began in reaction to the events between 1989 (the Eastern European revolutions) and 1991 (the demise of the Soviet Union) has been longer and in some ways more difficult than it might have been had there been greater individual and collective clairvoyance on the subject.

We can think about change in two different ways. The first is to look at change structurally in terms of relations among states. The three faces of such change include changes in the distribution of power among members of the system, changes in the relative nature of effective power within the system, and changes in the underlying dynamics in the system itself. The second is to try to describe the emerging patterns of the new system, for which purpose I will describe what I call a world of tiers.

The international system that evolved during the Cold War was a highly structured and, after a time, highly predictable set of relationships. The centerpiece of the system was the competition between the communist and noncommunist worlds, the main attraction of which was Soviet-American rivalry. That competition dominated national-security concerns and was the major datum in determining European and East Asian relations. It also spilled over into the old Third World, in which there evolved a competition for influence between the superpowers that in turn created a framework within which the internal and international behavior of Third World states was regulated (and, possibly most important for present purposes, violence was modulated and moderated—a point to which we will return).

Distribution of Power

That framework, of course, is no longer relevant or descriptive. The effective distribution of power within the international system has changed in at least four consequential ways. The first and most obvious change is the disappearance of the old Second (communist) World, meaning the removal from the field of play of the major ideological antagonist to Western physical and ideological dominance. (China remains technically communist but no longer promotes the ideology.) The states that once formed the opposition are now suitors seeking to join the prosperous states that constitute the major powers of the new order. The major question we have about our old adversaries, especially the Soviet successor states and the formerly communist states of Eastern and Central Europe, is the pace at which various of them will be allowed to join in the greater prosperity.

The second obvious change is that there is only one remaining superpower, the United States, and it is a superpower without any obvious rival for global leadership. This does not, of course, imply that the United States is a hegemonic power capable of imposing its will on the rest of the world. Indeed, one of the ways in which the new system is different is in how superpower status can be defined. During the Cold War, superpower status was largely defined in military, and especially thermonuclear, terms. As I will argue, this definition is no longer adequate, mostly because military power is no longer influential in a broad array of relationships, particularly those involving the major economic powers. Instead, superpower status must be modified to mean a state that has the broadest array of traditional instruments of national power (economic, military, diplomatic) available to it and that is accorded the highest status by other members of the system. Because the United States is the country that has the most, and most diverse, forms of power, and because the American system of political democracy and market economy currently has great appeal (what Joseph S. Nye Jr. calls soft power), it is the remaining superpower. The implications of that status will be explored in particular depth when we consider systemic responses to the new internal wars.

A third change in the distribution of power is that there is essentially only one power bloc in existence. That bloc is more or less coterminus with the Western alliance system (including Japan) but its status is more largely defined in economic terms. Membership is confined to the most economically advanced, market-based political democracies, which cumulatively constitute the expanding global economy and which I describe collectively as the First Tier. The vast majority of effective power within the emerging system resides within the members of the First Tier, although not all states of consequence (notably China and Russia) are members. (How and whether to incorporate the giants of the former communist world is a major systemic question and problem.)

The fourth and final change in the distribution of power is that there is great accord between the major powers that constitute the

First Tier. It is, for instance, virtually impossible to think of the possibility of armed conflict among any members of the First Tier. There is a political and economic like-mindedness between the major powers that has not been achieved (or even approximated) since the eighteenth century, when the European world was ruled by like-minded absolute monarchies and economic mercantilists.

This basic accord affects the nature of power in the evolving system. In the Cold War, military power was clearly preeminent, although the growth of an increasingly obvious disparity in productivity between the communist and capitalist worlds was adding an economic dimension as well. During the Cold War, the common security concern of capitalist countries was opposition to communist expansion; with that problem removed, they lack an obvious shared security focus.

Relative Nature of Power

Economic factors are becoming more important in the relations among states, whereas the applicability and effectiveness of military force is becoming more problematic. The countries of the First Tier overwhelmingly have the greatest military capability, and despite cutbacks on military spending, advanced capabilities that result from the application of the most advanced technologies (which are produced and hence controlled by the most advanced countries) to military capability (the so-called Revolution in Military Affairs, or RMA) will widen that gap. The most consequential states outside the First Tier, Russia and China, certainly have great power (the Russians, after all, do maintain the Soviet Union's arsenal of nuclear weapons), but it is not clear what would motivate either to attack the most advanced states, given that they are the key to Russia and China's economic betterment.

This disparity in military power between the market-based advanced democracies and the rest of the world is difficult to translate into usable influence. Within the relations among the countries of the First Tier, military power is irrelevant to influencing one another's behavior—the threat by the United States to take military action against Japan if it does not relent on terms of trade is laughable, for instance.

Military force *is* plausible in the old Third World (what I will describe as the Second Tier). However, two factors limit the application of military force by First Tier states in the Second Tier. The first limitation is what I call the *interest-threat mismatch:* In those places that involve substantial American (and other major power) interests there are no longer any major (or interesting) threats; the threat structure disappeared with the end of the Cold War. But there *are* threats (as in outbreaks of violence) in the old Third World, where there are not many important American interests. Thus, the interest-threat mismatch describes a situation in which the interests of the major powers are hardly threatened, and where the threats that do exist are hardly interesting.

This mismatch is vital to understanding likely systemic reaction (or the absence thereof) to the new internal wars. All of the major powers that might intervene in these affairs are political democracies; the major limitation on the application of military force in political democracies is public opinion, and it is difficult to convince free publics to put themselves and their countries at physical risk when important interests are not present. Thus, the combination of the interest-threat mismatch and the need for popular support for military action makes it questionable that the major powers will react to violence in Second Tier conflicts—with the possible and notable exceptions of humanitarian relief operations and true peacekeeping operations after fighting has ended. These exceptions are possible because the hideousness of many of these conflicts cries out for a helping hand, which can be extended with limited risk and expense.

The other limitation on applying major-power force in Second Tier conflicts is its relevance to the kinds of conflicts I am describing. It is not at all clear, for instance, that the electronic sophistication possessed by major-power armed forces is of much relevance to a conflict such as the criminal insurgencies in Sierre Leone and the sometimes-ended conflict in Liberia. In fact, computer-based wizardry may simply delude its possessors into believing they can do things for which their prowess is irrelevant. One is reminded that the North Vietnamese leader Tranh Van Duong, speaking of the American use of computers in the Vietnam conflict, argued that the speed at which computers work simply magnifies the possibility and pace of human stupidity.

I argue that Western militaries (among others) do not understand the nature of these conflicts, that dusting off Vietnam-era notions of insurgency and counterinsurgency (as is largely being done) is an inadequate and inappropriate way to narrow the understanding gap, and, further, that Western forces are not trained, equipped, or doctrinally prepared to become involved in most of these situations. (This should be one of the real lessons of the Somali experience for the United States.) The U.S. military, through such constructs as operations other than war (OOTW) and peace operations, is attempting to come to grips with these kinds of problems; as I will suggest in Chapter 5, it still has a long way to go.

The Rise of Economic Power

The other way in which power has changed in the new international system, as noted, is the rising importance of economic factors in international relations. For economic purposes, the world is essentially divided into two groups of states: the First Tier of wealthy market-based democracies, and the rest of the world, which economically lags behind by varying degrees. This was, of course, the case during the Cold War (although with the addition of a series of socialist economies that have all but disappeared); the current situation is, however, different in two fundamental ways.

The first major difference is in the degree of economic intertwining and intermingling among the economies of the countries of the First Tier. Thanks to dynamics such as the high-technology revolution in computing and telecommunications (increasingly the two are becoming a single industry), the most prosperous countries are part of an emerging single globalizing economy based upon basic precepts of market economics combined with a commitment to political democracy. In this economy, the level of interdependence and interconnection among firms and industries is great and growing, and it fuels the general prosperity of all the members (a positive-sum game). Conversely, this interdependence also means that downturns in one or more member economies are felt by all members. Moreover, the dynamics of the globalizing economy are making the gap between members and outsiders progressively wider.

The second major difference is in the nearly universal desire by those outside the global economy to become a part of it. Since 1989, virtually all the formerly communist states have renounced socialism as the basis for their economies. China, the last remaining major communist power, actively renounces socialism and trumpets the virtues of its capitalist Special Economic Zones (SEZs), which are providing the fuel for the world's fastest-growing economy. Vietnam's normalization of relations with the United States was in large measure motivated by the desire to increase the amount of investment by foreign corporations in the country. Although the transition to market economics has proven tortuous in a number of formerly communist countries because their legal and commercial systems are inimical to the structural change (Russia is a prime example of this problem), the only advocates of the socialist system are those two economic pile drivers, North Korea and Cuba. Even Cuba has instituted limited forms of private enterprise (private truck gardens to produce vegetables for instance), and the North Koreans eye the South Korean prosperity with increasingly open envy.

The market has extended elsewhere. The statism (practice of government ownership or regulation of industry) that for so long crippled economic growth in Latin America is breaking down in a wave of privatization, and the extension of the North American Free Trade Agreement (NAFTA) to other parts of the region will almost certainly accelerate the process even further.

Two parts of the world stand conspicuously outside this process. The most prominent is most of Africa, which is excluded because it has little in market or productive terms to offer to the system and is thus not attractive to the private enterprises that are the backbone of the global economy. The other is central and southern Asia. The Islamic areas of Asia cannot embrace the values of market-based democracy without secularization, because many of the values underpinning the capitalist system are anathema to the Islamic faith (the charging of interest, for instance, is considered usury). At the same time, parts of southern Asia are engulfed in domestic violence that impedes the orderly movement to a more prosperous condition, and other states (Nepal, for instance) are simply very poor and underdeveloped.

Possibly the most significant manifestations of the dynamics of the global economy occurred, with little public fanfare or analysis, in November 1994. In a suburb of Djakarta, Indonesia, the heads of state of the eighteen members of the Asia-Pacific Economic Cooperation (APEC) agreed in principle to authorize the drawing of a treaty among themselves that would create an APEC-wide free-trade area by the year 2020. (In the interim, the First Tier member states—the United States, Japan, Canada, Australia, and New Zealand—would institute a free-trade area by the year 2010.) Then in December, in Miami, the thirty-four Western Hemisphere states with democratically elected governments (all the states of the hemisphere except Cuba) also agreed in principle to authorize the drafting of a treaty to create a Free Trade Area of the Americas. (The fact that President Bill Clinton, an avid free trader, was a driving force at both meetings is not coincidental.)

Neither of these initiatives has yet turned into a binding agreement, and it may even be that neither of them will ever become reality. They are, nonetheless, potentially of enormous significance for the evolving international system. First, they encompass a great deal of the world's economic might; a condition of free trade among the parties would be a major force for further globalizing the economy into one large free-trade area. Second, if both come into being, they would almost certainly effect a single free-trade area, because four states (Canada, Chile, Mexico, and the United States) are members of both. If one adds the European Union to this array of regional economic powers, one has encompassed almost all of the most prosperous countries, while simultaneously providing a mechanism by which other states can aspire to the general prosperity.

The emergence of a global economy among advanced political democracies creates a like-mindedness among the major powers that has not existed for at least two centuries. Although the commitment to market economics and political democracy is not universal, there are few viable alternatives: There are still thug regimes in the world, but they are fewer in number and unextolled even by their practitioners. Moreover, by now it should be adequately established that one characteristic of political democracies is that they do not fight one another. This is true partly because they have little to fight over (since they share basic political and economic values) and partly because advanced industrial democracies rarely choose to attack one another. Because essentially all the most important states in the system are part of this general phenomenon, it follows that the dangers of a system-threatening conflict are essentially nonexistent. The only physical threat to the system is currently posed by Russian (or more remotely, Chinese) nuclear weapons, but it requires a considerable stretch of the imagination to find a motivation for carrying out such a threat. (Chinese saber-rattling over the Taiwanese election is an exception.) Reducing the threat even further, of course, forms much of the rationale for promoting Russian and Chinese economic and political development toward the First Tier.

At the same time, there is a great deal of violence and instability within the overall international system. That violence, however, is centered in the Second Tier of states, and especially in those areas most remote, both financially and geographically, from the global economy. An international system primarily concerned with economic matters (defining its most important interests in economic terms) may or may not concern itself with ameliorating violence outside the global economy.

Critical to my analysis of the nature of the evolving system is the notion of a world of tiers. Defining the tiers and, in the case of the Second Tier, the subtiers, is crucial to understanding the pattern of new internal war.

A WORLD OF TIERS

One of the major difficulties of understanding the contemporary international system derives from trying to describe the membership of the system in monolithic terms. It is difficult, even impossible in many cases, to generalize about the behavior of all states; as Singer and Wildavsky presciently described the problem in *The Real World Order,* "if you try to talk about the world as a whole, all you get is falsehoods and platitudes" (p. 3).

The problem, as Singer and Wildavsky were among the first to account, is that the world is, at a minimum, divided into two distinct parts, which they call the "zones of peace" and the "zones of turmoil." The former, which I call the First Tier, is composed roughly of the Organization of Economic Cooperation and Development (OECD): Canada and the United States in North America, the European Economic Area, Japan, Australia, and New Zealand. The "zones of turmoil," on the other hand, encompasses the rest of the world, most of which wishes to join the First Tier. I call this part of the world the Second Tier, and in recognition of its diversity, divide it into four subtiers that are useful descriptively and, more important for present purposes, for distinguishing between those areas more and less susceptible to internal and other violence. The two tiers are distinct.

The First Tier

The First Tier consists of the most advanced political democracies, all of which also have advanced, market-based economic systems. The result of this combination of economic and political freedom is what Singer and Wildavsky call *quality economies,* "a highly productive citizenry operating a complex information-intensive economy" (p. 14). They contend that the two factors are interactive: "The fact that essentially all wealthy countries are democracies is strong evidence that: (1) something about being wealthy makes a country likely to become democratic; (2) democracy may be necessary (or almost necessary) to become wealthy; or (3) both" (p. 17).

This description has been subject to criticism from a variety of quarters. The most basic objection is to its ethnocentrism: It is quintessentially Western, and more specifically, American. As such, the theory is vulnerable to the same charges of cultural bias as were theories of economic and political development devised in the 1950s and 1960s. Moreover, theories of cultural difference, like Samuel P.

Huntington's "clash of civilizations" thesis, show that Western notions are likely to run afoul of deeply held values of other civilizations. The most often cited examples of this incompatibility, of course, are those countries most devoutly (which is to say fundamentally) Islamic; some Asian cultures (especially those influenced by China) are often seen as resistant to Western political forms. As Singapore's Lee Kuan Yew stated in *Foreign Affairs* in March/April 1994, the West cannot "foist their system indiscriminately on societies in which it will not work" (p. 110).

Recognizing that there are discernible historical differences among different societies and cultures, I would contend that entirely too much is made of this purported societal exclusivity. Rather, it should be clear to observers that the most advanced countries are becoming increasingly homogenous: A shopping mall in China looks strikingly like its equivalent in Minneapolis, and the basic political values in most advanced countries are shared. The dual values of political and economic freedom are exceedingly powerful and universal in their appeal. To deny this self-evident truth is to engage in a kind of self-denigrating, even self-flagellating reverse ethnocentrism that distorts the fact that most of the world either shares or aspires to basic Western, even (dare to say) American values and living conditions. This does not imply "the end of history" (in Francis Fukuyama's term), in which these ideas will predominate forever, but to argue that they do not predominate today is simply wrongheaded.

A more basic criticism of the quality-economy idea is that it is not universal even in those states where it is said to exist. Not all (or even a majority of) Americans are highly self-motivated because they are economically free to make their own decisions; a lot of people are stuck in dead-end jobs over which they have little control and that do not inspire them to the kind of creative endeavor that allows quality economies to outperform less-quality economies. Although there is some validity to this criticism, it too misses the mark. The point is not that everyone participates in the quality economy but that more people do than in lesser economies, thereby making the quality economies in net superior. The more-productive members of a quality economy, in other words, are more productive than their counterparts in a nonquality economy, and the result is a more productive overall economy.

What distinguishes the countries of the First Tier is their basic homogeneity of political and economic outlook and their joint—and mutually beneficial—participation in the global economy. Such conflict as exists among them is at the margins of their basic relationships and does not threaten the central benefits they enjoy. As noted earlier, the result is that conflict, and more specifically war, among any of the states of the First Tier is essentially unthinkable.

The Second Tier

The same is not the case of the much more diverse Second Tier. It covers a vast array of states and conditions, from very advanced countries such as Asia's four tigers (South Korea, Hong Kong, Singapore, and Taiwan), which are poised to join the First Tier, to exceedingly poor countries whose near- or even medium-term prospects of becoming meaningful members of the broader prosperity are minimal.

The subtiers of the Second Tier are classified according to a scheme that is heavily economic in its content (although not in entirely conventional ways), but with a political content as well. The economic component is based largely in the structures of various economies, conceptualized through the idea of advancement through the various industrial revolutions. These are summarized in Table 1.1.

Table 1.1 Industrial Revolutions and Developmental Status

Industrial-Revolution Status	Primary Economic Activities
Pre-First (Traditional)	Subsistence agriculture, natural-resources extraction, cottage industry
First (Heavy Industry)	Heavy industrial goods (e.g., steel), some consumer goods
Second (Service)	Sophisticated consumer goods, licensure, services
Third (Information)	Knowledge, Research and Development, new processes and products

The distinctions are straightforward. The least-developed economies have the least sophisticated means of production, either production for personal consumption (subsistence agriculture), production for the immediate community (cottage industry), or mineral or other extraction. The first industrial revolution begins the sophistication of economy by introducing heavy industries such as iron and steel (what we now talk about as the "sunset" industries of the "rust belt"). Further sophistication results in a reorientation toward more sophisticated goods and services, and the current cutting edge is the information-based revolution. The contours of a fourth industrial revolution have not yet appeared clearly on the horizon. Some would argue that the economic restructuring after the first revolution is "postindustrial" and that the changes are economic or productive revolutions.

These criteria are clearly developmental and reflect varying degrees of sophistication and wealth: People in a country that has undergone the Third Industrial Revolution are likely to be better off than those in a Second Industrial Revolution country, for instance. Moreover, the more advanced the country's economic structure is, the more likely it is to achieve the economic and political quality that results in a more productive, self-motivated work force, which in turn promotes greater economic advancement.

The political criterion of subtier classification is the existence of political democracy and the stability of democratic forms measured by the ability to sustain democracy through governmental succession. This criterion admittedly is subject to the criticism of cultural bias as overly Western, but nonetheless it is congruent with the need to achieve the motivations necessary for a quality economy. It may be possible, as indeed has been the case in a number of Asian countries, to engage in considerable economic progress while maintaining an authoritarian political form. The argument has been made, for instance, that in Singapore tyranny is popular and thus the criterion of Western-style political democracy is irrelevant, and even demeaning and unfair. This argument may be, for the time being, of some validity; I do not believe it will be over the longer run. The people of Singapore (and China and elsewhere) will demand political freedom that will look strikingly like the political freedom enjoyed in the First Tier.

These criteria are as much suggestive as they are precise. Measuring the composition of economies is difficult, because any economy will contain elements of the more primitive economic activities from which it has evolved to its current status. A country that has undergone the First Industrial Revolution, for instance, is likely to have steel mills sitting next to subsistence farms; even the most intensely information-based societies will have extractive industries as part of their economic mix. The criterion is based on the cutting edge and relative mix. Inevitably, some systems will be on the borderline, at which point more or less subjective judgments have to be employed, but it was my experience, as reflected in the application of the classification scheme found in the Appendix, that there were relatively few difficult calls. At the same time, it should be noted that each category represents a range of characteristics rather than a monolith—within the lowest Second Tier subtier of developable states, for instance, there are very poor and industrially undeveloped states as well as states in the process of entering the First Industrial Revolution.

With this background in mind, we can define the basic tiers and subtiers. The First Tier can be defined most easily and succinctly. What distinguishes First Tier states is that they have entered the Third or High-Technology Revolution, which is increasingly the driving force behind their economic growth and prosperity. Not only do the states of the First Tier enjoy the fruits of high technology, but they also *produce* that technology. Because so much of the technology is based in the inherently international telecommunications area, and because so much technological activity is conducted by private multinational corporations, the very process contributes to the globalizing impact of the international economy among participants. The other distinguishing characteristic of First Tier states is their demonstrated, continuous commitment to political democracy.

Subtiers of the Second Tier

The diverse Second Tier can best be understood as a series of subtiers, each with somewhat different characteristics. These differentiations, as they are related to primary economic activity in the different industrial revolutions, are captured in Table 1.2.

Table 1.2 Industrial Revolutions and Tiers

Industrial-Revolution Status	Tier/Subtier
Pre-First (Traditional)	Developable Second Tier
First (Heavy Industry)	Partially Developed Second Tier
Second (Service)	Developed Second Tier
Third (Information)	First Tier

The table reveals three of the four subtiers in a developmental sequence from least to most closely resembling the First Tier. In order to discuss the subtiers, however, I reverse that order and add the fourth subtier, which consists of the resource-rich countries (mostly those with great petroleum wealth) that do not fit neatly into any of the developmentally arranged subtiers and stand aside as a special case.

The first subtier is the *developed subtier.* It consists of those states that have successfully mastered the requisites of basic industrialization (heavy industry) or have managed to bypass that stage and enter instead the second industrial revolution of sophisticated manufacture and the provision of services. Countries in this category may be active consumers and even approximate producers of the high technology that would elevate them to First Tier status. Because this category shares with the other subtiers a range of developmental levels, some are closer to becoming members of the First Tier than others.

Countries of the developed subtier are concentrated in East Asia and Latin America. The states closest to First Tier status are found in the Pacific Rim of East Asia, notably South Korea, Taiwan, Hong Kong, and Singapore. Korea will likely prove the prototype for states making the transition from the Second to the First Tier: It is already the leading ship-building state in the world, and its electronics industry is fast becoming a technology producer. The movement of Hong Kong toward or into the First Tier is clouded by its impending merger with China in 1997. The more autonomous Hong Kong is allowed to remain, the better its chances of achieving First Tier status (assuming that capital flight from the colony is not accompanied by "intellectual flight" as well). Singapore's authoritarian system is, in the long run, incompatible with developing a true quality economy, and the form of association that evolves between Taiwan and mainland China makes its future at least partially problematic. (One intriguing possibility is that the prosperous parts of eastern and southern China [the SEZs] will break away from the rest of China after the current ruling gerentocracy dies off and form a new state with Hong Kong, Macao, and Taiwan—a combination with the potential of being an economic juggernaut.)

The other concentration of developed Second Tier states is in Latin America, although these states are generally more economically removed from the First Tier than are the Asian tigers. This group includes Argentina, Brazil, Chile, Mexico, and Venezuela. All have growing economies and at least fragile democracies. Whether (or how) the Western Hemisphere regional free-trade process occurs will affect the upward movement of these states. An encouraging sign in these and other Latin American states is declining statism and the increased privatization of economic activity. Other developed Second Tier states include South Africa, Israel, Cyprus, and Slovenia.

The second subtier of the Second Tier is the *partially developed sub-*

tier. States in this category have made some progress through the First Industrial Revolution, and isolated sectors of their economies may have advanced even further. At the same time, the states in this subtier generally have substantial segments of the economy engaged in the kinds of subsistence agriculture and extractive industry associated with preindustrial societies. Politically, states in the partially developed category include well-established democracies (India), fragile democracies (a number of Latin American countries), systems evolving toward democracy (a number of the formerly communist Eastern European countries), and a number of undemocratic states (China).

The most prominent partially developed states are China and India. By some measures, China is the most economically dynamic country in the world. It already represents the world's second-largest economy in terms of total buying power, and its economy has been (or among) the fastest growing in the world. At the same time, this growth and dynamism is physically limited to the south and east within China, whereas large parts of the interior remain basically pre-First Industrial Revolution. The Chinese Communist Party maintains a monopoly of political power to prevent, it claims, a Soviet-style balkanization that would accompany democratization. (A breakup of China such as I suggested earlier is not unlikely under any circumstances.) China's abysmal human-rights record is a well-documented matter that the regime hardly tries to conceal except at selected international events, such as the UN conference on women's rights hosted at Beijing in 1995.

India is also an anomaly. Its large middle class (about 100 million people) is expanding rapidly, and its growing technological class (mostly educated overseas) is becoming a competitor to more generally advanced countries in areas such as the design and manufacture of computer chips, often under licensure arrangements with First Tier firms. At the same time, large portions of the Indian population remain at subsistence level at best. Politically, India remains one of the Second Tier's original democracies, but it is simultaneously beset by a variety of secessionists who would separate parts of putatively Indian territory from the country (the princely states of Jammu and Kashmir being the most obvious examples).

The third subtier is the *developable subtier.* Numerically it is the largest subtier, containing slightly more than half of the countries of the Second Tier. Like the other subtiers, its members are diverse; it includes a number of states almost at the level of partially developed states, but ranges downward to a number of states whose economies are so undeveloped and whose prospects for development are so slender that it is difficult to be optimistic about their likelihood of economic success even in the long term. Most of the states in this category are also nondemocratic, the major exceptions being former British colonies such as Sri Lanka.

The states in this subtier are geographically concentrated. Thirty-six are in Africa, nineteen are formerly communist states (the former Soviet Union and Eastern Europe, especially the Balkans), and seventeen are in Asia, principally in southern Asia and Micronesia.

The final subtier is the *resource-rich subtier.* It represents a category that does not fit into the developmental sequence of the other three subtiers. What distinguishes the countries of the resource-rich subtier is that they are generally quite wealthy, but their wealth is derived not from activity associated with progression through the industrial revolutions but almost exclusively from the exploitation of petroleum resources. The world's addiction to petroleum-based energy has bestowed great wealth on these societies, but except for their financial sectors they are all relatively underdeveloped. (A litmus test to distinguish the oil-rich countries from the rest is to see what their economic structures would look like if petroleum revenue were removed.)

Politically, all the countries in this category except Trinidad and Tobago are nondemocratic. Not surprisingly, the greatest concentration of states is in the Middle East, notably the Persian/Arabian Gulf littoral, and in northern Africa. Trinidad, Tobago, and Brunei are the other members. A number of states (Nigeria and Venezuela, for instance) that derive much of their wealth from oil are not included because they have other economic sectors that qualify them for inclusion in the developmental sequence of Second Tier states.

The distribution of states in the Second Tier is summarized in Table 1.3.

Table 1.3 Second Tier Subtiers by Region

	Developed	Partially Developed	Developable	Resource-rich	Total
Asia, Pacific	4	8	17	1	30
Middle East	2	6	2	7	17
Latin America	5	19	8	1	33
Former communist (USSR, Eastern Europe)	1	8	19	0	28
Africa	1	11	36	4	52
Total	13	52	82	13	160

The most notable aspect of this distribution, for the purpose of dealing with violence in the system, is the location of the least-developed states: in most of Africa (which includes by far the largest number), parts of southern Asia and Micronesia, and the formerly communist states that were once part of the Soviet Union or Eastern Europe. These states share two characteristics that are entirely noncoincidental. First, they are in the areas that lie principally outside the growing global economy and, more to the point, those defined by the three evolving regional free-trade blocs. Second, it is in these areas that most of the internal violence in the post–Cold War world is occurring. These two factors go a long way toward explaining the patterns of violence in the contemporary system.

CONCLUSIONS: INTERNATIONAL RELATIONS AND VIOLENCE IN A WORLD OF TIERS

The evolving world of tiers bears conceptual similarities and dissimilarities to the Cold War system in the ways it operates and in the pattern of violence associated with it. The distribution of wealth within the system remains uneven, some would say inequitable. What is changing is the increasing emergence of a global economy, whose roots go back at least to the 1980s, that increasingly separates the wealthy from the rest. The virtual disappearance of Marxism-Leninism as an operational and even an ideological opponent to Western notions of economy and politics is striking, because it leaves us for the time being with no real intellectual alternative to the Western way of organizing the international system. One need not be either hyperbolic or xenophobic to observe the "unipolar moment" (Charles Krauthammer's term) of the conceptual ascendancy of the Western system of market economy and political democracy.

What does this ascendancy mean for organizing the international system and for dealing with the residue of violence and instability that characterizes what some have argued is a more disorderly world than the one it supercedes? The generally unopposed tranquillity and orderliness within the First Tier that is the principal improvement of the system to date has not been matched in the Second Tier, which is arguably more unstable than it was before. Understanding the implications of this imbalance depends upon three questions. The first is how the interaction between the most developed states and the old Third World has changed with the end of the Cold War. The second question is how, and whether, the countries of the First Tier will deal with the problems of the Second Tier (most notably its lower subtiers). Third, there is the question of what to do about the pattern of mostly internal violence within the Second Tier that is the principal blight on the more general peace of the First Tier.

Intertier Relations?

During the Cold War, the role of most of the old Third World was peripheral to the major activity of the international system. The states that emerged from colonial rule were almost uniformly poor and unproductive, lacking great intrinsic value to the major powers unless they happened to possess energy, some mineral abundance, or strategic geographical features such as maritime choke points. The problems of individual Third World states or even regions therefore ranked relatively low on the geopolitical agendas of the major powers.

Such interest that did evolve was instrumental as an extension of the East-West competition to the emerging Third World. What began as a competition to turn more parts of the world red or blue (communist or noncommunist), through such devices as mutual security treaties, evolved into a competition more narrowly focused on currying influence through arms transfers and other forms of economic and military assistance. As often as not, the purpose of the competition was as much to deny access to the other side as it was to gain some advantage for either the Soviets or the Americans (or occasionally the Chinese).

Although this form of competition could be viewed as a cynical sideshow to the greater Soviet-American confrontation that was the centerpiece of the Cold War international system, it was not without its positive effects in terms of creating some level of stability in areas that might otherwise have been more unstable. The extension of the Cold War created a level of interest in Third World regions and countries where no apparent interest previously existed. Once they entered the competition, both the Soviet Union and the United States quickly recognized an interest in moderating their "clients'" behavior, at least to the extent of ensuring that relations between enemies did not become so murderous as to drag the two sponsors into direct military confrontation. Currying influence in the Third World was clearly a part of the Cold War game; it was not, however, worth the risk of World War III. This was the lesson learned from such disparate events as the Yom Kippur War, the Cuban missile crisis, and various of the Indo-Pakistani conflicts, all of which produced at least fleeting prospects of direct Soviet-American confrontation. The result was an incentive to influence the affairs of Third World client states.

For better or worse, one of the apparent motives of the Soviet Union in initiating the changes that ended the Cold War was the financial debilitation created by competition in the Third World. When Mikhail Gorbachev wrote in 1987 in *Perestroika* (especially Chapter 5) that he wanted to see an end of the competition in the Third World (and hardly anybody believed him at the time), he was admitting that the Soviets simply could no longer afford the economic drain of albatrosses like Afghanistan, Angola, Mozambique, Cuba, and Nicaragua. Even before the formal dissolution of the Soviet state with the last tick of the clock in 1991, the Soviets had distanced themselves from most of the Third World. Russia has continued this progressive disengagement, focusing what foreign activism as it has left on the states of the "near abroad" (the former Soviet republics) and on its efforts to attract foreign support for its conversion to a market economy.

Because the primary basis of American interest in many Third World areas (most of Africa south of the Sahara and north of South Africa as a prime example) was to counter Soviet interest, the removal of the Soviets leaves the United States with hardly any interests on which to exert its energies. As a result, the United States has progressively removed itself from regions of the Second Tier.

This withdrawal has had both positive and negative effects. In some cases it has appeared to stimulate resolution of older conflicts. In the Arab-Israeli conflict, for example, the Americans remained engaged and Israel's rivals had no alternate source of support in opposing solutions brokered by the United States. The Indo-Pakistani conflict has become more muted, and the withdrawal of Soviet support for insurgents in places as diverse as Angola and El Salvador has likewise led to resolutions of ongoing bloody wars.

Where both sides have withdrawn from areas, constraints appear to have been removed. There is no outside power with a systematic presence or influence in much of central Africa, for instance. Occasionally the French or other European powers will become involved in former colonies where they retain some interest, but such influence is insufficient to constrain governments or rebellious factions. It is, of course, arguable that not even Cold War levels of involvement would have affected the civil strife in such places as Liberia (whose problems date back to well before the end of the Cold War), but the coincidence of outsider withdrawal and the emergence of virtual chaos is striking nonetheless.

If parts of the Second Tier, and especially its generally poorest areas, are beset by developmental problems that contribute to violence and instability in some cases, what, if anything, should the countries of the First Tier be prepared to do? The question becomes especially important when those problems spill over into gory episodes, as in Rwanda in the spring of 1994. A traditional analysis based on the calculation of vital interests suggests that where threats and interests are misaligned in those parts of the world outside the globalizing economy, there is certainly not much worth fighting over. Only an expansion of the definition of interest to encompass "vital humanitarian interests," as Boutros-Ghali has extolled, would create the rationale for involvement in areas clearly on the periphery. In the Rwandan case the major powers took almost no action to prevent or moderate the slaughter; their response was largely limited to improving the plight of refugees through humanitarian relief efforts and to organizing a war-crimes tribunal. At least part of the reason for this was that democratic publics in the First Tier would support no further action; moreover, no one had a very good idea of how to stop the slaughter once it began.

We are left with a dichotomy with which we will probably not be entirely comfortable. The globalizing economy and its manifestations in such entities as the free-trade areas and economic unions may provide a mechanism to reach down to states throughout the developmental hierarchy and draw them into the general prosperity and tranquillity. The European Union can, and may, reach out to the formerly communist states of Eastern Europe and even the former Soviet Union itself. Candidates include countries in all the developmental subtiers of the Second Tier, and the proposed free-trade areas of APEC and the Western Hemisphere contain states that run the developmental gamut.

Those states that fall outside the actual and potential ranks of the global economy form the uncomfortable part of the dichotomy. Covering most of Africa, and parts of central and southern Asia, these are among the poorest states in the world, and they hold little interest for the private concerns that drive the global economy. What appeal, for instance, do desperately poor Nepal or war-torn Sierre Leone or Tajikistan have for huge multinational corporations like Philips and IBM?

Yet it is these places that represent the principal sources of turmoil in the post–Cold War international system. Although the response of the First Tier to problems in these areas has so far been restrained at best, it is not clear what will happen if the current spate of violence becomes an epidemic. How many simultaneous Chechnyas, Bosnias, and Somalias is the system willing to tolerate?

At least part of the answer to this question concerns the limits of effective action that can be taken even if the desire to do so exists. The experience in Somalia certainly dampened American enthusiasm for outside involvement. The interjection of conventional U.S. forces could provide no more than a bandage to temporarily halt the physical violence and suffering stemming from the political anarchy of that land. One of the lessons of Somalia was that the United States was physically and conceptually unprepared for the kind of problem with which it was confronted.

The determination of whether or not the First Tier (and most particularly the United States as the principal military power) will attempt to moderate or influence Second Tier internal violence requires a thorough understanding of the dynamics of that violence. Much of the response to Second Tier violence has so far been concentrated within military establishments charged in a general way with devising strategies for these "operations other than war." The extent of this exercise has been to dust off and refine theories of insurgency and counterinsurgency originally devised after the Vietnam war. The following chapter begins to assess the applicability of such theories to the changing international system.

REFERENCES

Boutros-Ghali, Boutros. *An Agenda for Peace: Preventive Diplomacy, Peacemaking, and Peace-Keeping.* New York: United Nations, 1992.

———. "Empowering the United Nations." *Foreign Affairs* 72, 5 (Winter 1992/93): 89–102.

Fukuyama, Francis. "The End of History?" *National Interest* 16 (Summer 1989): 3–18.

Gorbachev, Mikhail S. *Perestroika: New Thinking for Our Country and the World.* New York: Harper and Row, 1987.

Gotlieb, Gidon. *Nation Against State: A New Approach to Ethnic Conflicts and the Decline of Sovereignty.* New York: Council on Foreign Relations Press, 1993.

Gurr, Ted Robert, and Barbara Harff. *Ethnic Conflict in World Politics.* Boulder, Colo.: Westview Press, 1994.

Huntington, Samuel P. "Clash of Civilizations." *Foreign Affairs* 72, 3 (Summer 1993): 22–49.

Moynihan, Daniel Patrick. *Pandaemonium: Ethnicity in World Politics.* New York: Oxford University Press, 1993.

Pfaff, William. *The Wrath of Nations: Civilization and the Furies of Nationalism.* New York: Simon and Schuster, 1993.

Singer, Max, and Aaron Wildavsky. *The Real World Order: Zones of Peace, Zones of Turmoil.* Chatham, N.J.: Chatham House, 1993.

Snow, Donald M. *The Shape of the Future: The Post–Cold War World* (Second Edition). Armonk, N.Y.: M. E. Sharpe, 1995.

Zakaria, Fareed. "A Conversation with Lee Kuan Yew." *Foreign Affairs* 73, 2 (March/April 1994): 109–126.

2

Underlying Causes of Internal War

"War is not merely a political act, but also a political instrument, a continuation of political relations, a carrying out of the same by other means." Carl von Clausewitz writes in his epochal *On War* to describe the relationship between war and the political purposes for which it is fought. Mao Zedong, the leading twentieth-century theoretician and practitioner of revolutionary warfare and himself a student of Clausewitz, concurred, stating succinctly in one of the speeches digested in his *Collected Works:* "War cannot be divorced from politics for a single moment."

If one accepts this conventional formulation of the function of war, including traditional internal war, then an exploration of organized armed violence must begin with the underlying political problems within or between states that lead one or more parties to take recourse to arms as the only way to resolve their differences. Not only must one understand what gave rise to the decision to enter into violence; if peace is to be reinstituted in some way acceptable to all parties and hence to produce a "better state of the peace" (in Sir Basil Liddell Hart's phrase), those conditions acceptable to all must also be known. To become involved in war without understanding these dynamics, either as participant, observer, or, most cogently for our purposes, as potential outside intervener, is to risk the irrelevance or failure of the effort.

This formulation, especially as applied to modern conflict, has not always been part of the American way of looking at war, and it is not clear that the Clausewitzian formulation is entirely appropriate for describing contemporary reality—and especially the new internal wars that are central to our concern. Viewing war as an explicitly political event, particularly within the professional military of the

United States, is a fairly recent phenomenon. In large measure it is the result of trying to learn the lessons of the war in Vietnam, when the failure of the top military and political leadership fully to appreciate the political realities in that country and the practical improbability of American success given those realities, contributed to the failure of the enterprise. Aided by the publication of Harry Summers's *On Strategy,* a thoroughly Clausewitzian critique of that war, the professional military—largely through the various war colleges—has become thoroughly Clausewitzian in the way it views the underlying causes of war, and almost as thoroughly Maoist in the way it views the dynamics of internal war.

The sophistication of this understanding of the political dynamics that lead to and result from war represents a considerable step forward for the U.S. military. It is an institution that has historically prided itself in its apoliticism and even glorified its aloofness from studying and understanding politics, as if the mere association were somehow demeaning. The potential problem, however, is that current events and dynamics may no longer be explainable in terms of Clausewitzian analysis. A number of observers argue that traditional warfare, such as that fought before the rise of the European state system (by the Vikings, Cossacks, or Mongols, for instance), was an autonomous activity devoid of any conscious connection to politics: We may be seeing a reversion to this "pre-Clausewitzian" style of war.

This point may best be made by analogy. For most analysts in the military and defense intellectual communities, the touchstone from which the evaluation of internal war situations begins is the Vietnam war. A whole literature that views internal war as a struggle for Lyndon Baines Johnson's "hearts and minds of men," where the contestants have identical "centers of gravity" (the loyalty of the population), has the war in Vietnam as its intellectual base, spruced up by strategic analysis and sprinkled with quotations from Mao and other revolutionaries. The underlying causes of conflict are similarly grounded in a body of literature that is based on theories of development crafted as decolonization occurred during the Cold War.

What if this mode of analysis is simply inapplicable in some or all of the instances of new internal war? Cold War–based frameworks probably were applicable in Somalia, which is why many in the military (at least privately), and many outside analysts, were so unenthusiastic about becoming involved in that tragic affair. In essence, no military action could deal with the real underlying problem: anarchy resulting from the inability of any clan or coalition of clans to impose order. A Clausewitzian analysis does very little to explain the rampage in Rwanda, wherein there was no ennobling political or ideological goal behind the slaughter (other than possibly serving to keep conservative Hutus in power), one could find no common center of gravity to which contending parties were attempting to appeal, and the rapaciousness of the violence violated all tenets of the theories of insurgency-counterinsurgency, grounded in the Maoist mobile-guerrilla model, that form the basis of our understanding of internal-war dynamics.

In Rwanda the Vietnam war analogy could not adequately explain what went on. If there was a parallel experience during the Cold War, it might have been the Khmer Rouge rampage in Cambodia between 1975 and 1978, at least in terms of the hideousness of the atrocities. But the fit there is imperfect: What the Khmer Rouge did to the Cambodian people was the act of a government—at least of sorts—putatively disciplining a recalcitrant segment of the population (anyone who disagreed with them). It is not clear what the Tutsis (and sympathetic Hutus) were to learn from the Hutu rampage other than to flee or die. It may be that the more appropriate analogy is the tribally based warfare of places like Angola or Mozambique, where ethnically defined political movements, aided by Cold War sponsors, vied for years for political control. Even there the slaughter was mitigated by what the sponsors would tolerate, a sign of some restraint not clearly evident in Rwanda.

Responding to post–Cold War internal wars with perspectives and strategies appropriate to Cold War situations is adequate if Cold War and post–Cold War conflicts are alike. If they are different, the old formulations may be inadequate or even misleading in ways that are difficult to specify in advance. It suggests a parallel with the old adage that the military always prepares for the last war.

This chapter examines the contemporary understanding of the underlying causes of conflict that lead to internal war. It begins with an analysis of the political dimension: What kinds of political circumstances may lead a group or groups to conclude that only armed violence will produce a just order in which they can pursue their self-interest? The discussion then turns to the economic dimension, specifically the kinds of economic conditions and developmental circumstances that appear to be more or less conducive to a political determination to initiate violence.

THE POLITICAL DIMENSION OF CHANGE

The political dimension of internal war has two aspects: the existence of a political situation deemed intolerable by some contending groups within the state, and contending visions of what the political situation should look like in the future (the better state of the peace). During the period of the Cold War the emphasis tended to be on the factors leading groups to go to war, given the generally presumed outcome of control of a sovereign government, normally described in communist-anticommunist terms. In the post–Cold War world some of that emphasis remains (why do movements start wars?) but there is less agreement on what constitutes better states of the peace.

The Cold War Pattern

The backdrop of Second Tier (then Third World) violence during the Cold War was the process and outcome of decolonization. That process created sovereign states where there had been dependencies of the major powers; internal conflict could then take the place of violence directed only at the colonizing power. Independence created a political landscape in newly sovereign states in which the rules were not clearly delineated nor the political actors schooled or experienced in manipulating the reins of power. The result was, in a number of instances, a recipe for disaster. Arguably, some of this dynamic remains in the post–Cold War world; one could consider the dissolution of the Soviet and Yugoslav states as a kind of decolonization process resulting in a series of newly independent states about as well prepared for independent rule as were their African and Asian counterparts during the Cold War period.

The Colonial Impact. Two points stand out from the colonial experience that bear directly on the internal problems of postcolonial polities. The first concerns the physical pattern that colonialism took. Generally speaking, the colonizing countries occupied and aggregated territories into colonial units with little care, and usually less understanding, of preexisting political, including ethnic, realities. In Africa, for instance, the general rule of thumb was that the colonizer would lay claim to a stretch of coastline and then extend rule inward. In the process, preexisting political boundaries were ignored where they were known. The Berlin Conference of 1883, in which the final colonial dissection of Africa was completed, took place without even accurate geographical maps of the continent, much less political or anthropological maps that would delineate tribal or other grounds. Moreover, the economics of scale suggested that larger colonial administrative units were better (more profitable) than smaller units, thereby maximizing the likelihood that arbitrary boundaries would violate preexisting patterns. This phenomenon was widespread in both Africa and the Islamic Middle East.

This pattern of colonization had two major effects that would carry over perniciously into the postcolonial experience. The first was that almost all the former colonies became multinational states wherein several distinct groups, which often were rivals before colonialism and reverted to rivalry after the colonial experience was over, tried to coexist. When independence was achieved, groups suspicious of one another on ethnic, tribal, religious, or other grounds were required to work out a modus vivendi for self-governance. The result too often was a fractious condition of nationally defined group competition for political power, often wielded at the expense of other groups. In a few instances (the Kurds of Iran, Iraq, Turkey, and Syria; the Ibo of Nigeria and Cameroons), new state boundaries divided national groups that sought statehood together (a phenomenon often referred to as irredentism), creating a further basis for dissension.

The second, and quite opposite, effect was economic. Whereas political integration was seldom encouraged among the population segments of colonies (reflecting the British principle of divide and rule to guard against the emergence of concerted anticolonial movements), some economic integration often did occur. Agricultural areas were sometimes developed to provide food for those working mines in another part of a colony, for instance. Large plantations in colonies required transportation systems in addition to what amounted to tenant labor.

The result was that, when independence was achieved, newly independent states were fairly often economically but not politically unified. In some cases it might have made sense to break colonial units into political entities that more accurately reflected previous realities or ethnic habitation, but such division conflicted with the economic infrastructure inherited from the colonial experience.

Another point to consider about the colonial experience was that it rarely prepared populations for self-governance after independence. If one starts from the premise (which is a fair one) that the purpose of colonies was profit rather than philanthropy, this stands to reason. Providing political and administrative training for subject populations—politicizing them, in other words—inevitably would lead to the emergence of political movements, one of whose likely purposes would be to end colonial rule. This, of course, was never the purpose of the colonizing governments or the private enterprises they brought with them. It would have been a violation of self-interest to train colonial populations in anything but the most menial of political and administrative tasks.

The consequences were predictable. As demands for independence began to sweep first across Asia in the 1940s (with roots going back to the 1920s and 1930s in some cases) and into Africa in the 1950s (as well as in the Caribbean and isolated parts of South America such as the Guianas), the uniform predicament was a lack of national preparation for self-rule, the absence of any sense of national unity or inclusionary nationalism (a fact often masked at the time by the general enthusiasm for expelling the Europeans), and, most important, a shortage of competent and honest leaders.

Although the exact pattern varied somewhat depending on the colonial ruler, the general condition was drearily the same. In most cases, natives who had been allowed political positions no higher than that of clerk were suddenly elevated to the status of administrators or became political leaders. Military forces that had been officered by Europeans suddenly had undereducated sergeants promoting themselves to flag rank. Uganda's Idi Amin Dada, with a fourth-grade education, comes to mind as a particularly vivid example. The citizens of the country who did have education adequate to take on leadership positions either were too few in number (Zaire, the former Belgian Congo, had only a handful of college graduates when it was granted independence) or were too tainted by association with the colonists to provide the critical mass necessary to develop the state.

The blame for this situation occupies its own literature. From the standpoint of the colonizing countries, the period after World War II presented them with unappealing choices. All the major colonial powers had been greatly weakened by the war and were under considerable pressure to pull back from overseas commitments they could no longer afford (while the purpose of colonies was to make money, most of them did not). Similarly, prestige motives ("great powers have colonies") became a luxury that could not be sustained: The sun was going to have to set on the British empire.

World War II had itself served as a stimulus for independence movements. Colonial subjects had been pressed into service for the mother country as soldiers or to replace factory workers off fighting the war. The experience often revealed the lack of universality of their suffering and exposed them to subversive ideas of political rights and independence from which their colonial rulers had generally tried to shield them. (The first editions of the great French political philosophers such as Montesquieu and Rousseau were smuggled into French Indochina in Chinese translations.) In the parts of East Asia conquered by Japan, the myth of European invincibility was effectively shattered. More basically, it was difficult to ask people to sacrifice personally and then willingly return to their bonds.

The choices for European countries facing independence movements were few and unpleasant. They could resist them, as did the French in Indochina and Algeria. Resistance often meant entanglement in bloody civil wars against independence movements employing some variant of the Maoist strategy and encouraged to varying degrees by one or the other of the major communist powers. Such involvements were generally protracted, bloody, unpopular among war-weary populations, and unsuccessful in the long run.

An alternative to resistance was to try to negotiate a period of transition during which the population, or at least a portion of it, could be prepared for self-rule. This approach provided at least the appearance of responsibility and the faint prospect of success: Responsible individuals could be identified and educated into the notion of responsible, democratic self-governance. The problem was that because essentially no preparation for self-government had been made, such a process would almost certainly take longer than populations yearning for independence would likely be willing to endure. Independence was an immediate demand.

The other option was to accede to demands for independence and hope for the best. This was the option chosen, for instance, by Belgium's King Leopold, who announced in 1959 that the Belgian Congo (a colony technically owned by the king) would be granted independence a year later, despite the fact that essentially no preparations for independence had been made. During the 1950s there was a standing joke that portrayed the British foreign minister traveling through the colonies with blank independence treaties that only required filling in the soon-to-be-independent state's name and the signature of a native.

Once a colonial power had adequately demonstrated (including to itself) the futility of armed resistance, the alternative was to give in and grant independence, usually with some apparent attempt to prepare the people for independence but with little realistic expectation of stability. The major exception was the Portuguese and their African possessions, which they did not relinquish until the middle 1970s; their colonies were much more integral to the Portuguese economy than was the case elsewhere.

The colonial powers have been roundly criticized for both the colonial experience and the way it ended. The most critical have been adherents of the so-called *dependencia* school, who have argued that the colonial experience brutalized and humiliated the populations on which it was imposed; manipulated, distorted, and retarded the economies and political development of those states; and left the postcolonial societies they had systematically exploited in a disadvantaged position. From this analysis, *dependencia* theorists and other supporters of the Second Tier conclude an obligation on the part of the First Tier aggressively to underwrite and promote economic and political development in the Second Tier. The same argument can be, and occasionally is, extended to the obligation to become involved in Second Tier internal wars that have their roots in the way colonies were divested.

One need not take any particular position on the *dependencia* construction for present purposes. The colonial experience was undoubtedly brutal and denigrating. (George Orwell's little-known *Burmese Days* provides a particularly chilling depiction of that experience.) But its direct relevance to the present is questionable. A few challenge the assertion that the colonial period distorted and retarded Third World economic development, arguing that in the absence of European intrusion most developing-world countries would have remained even more primitive traditional societies. Whether the colonial powers could have accomplished decolonization any differently is also debatable. What obligations the process creates is a moral question.

Results of Decolonization. The principal concern of this discussion is the result of the decolonizing process. Most of the newly independent countries adopted political forms that were democratic, usually based on some modification of the constitution of the former colonizer. Unfortunately, except in a few cases, the political elite and the population lacked the sophistication to master and operate a democratic system (which is, by virtue of its emphasis on providing choices rather than directions, a more difficult kind of system to operate than a less democratic system).

In the worst cases the result was a cycle of instability that continues today. Those who rode independence to power often appeared inept, incapable of providing the benefits that were supposed to accrue from statehood, or corrupt and venal. The most common problems were inadequate experience at governing, underestimation of the depth of problems at hand, and inadequate resources to deal with the problems that citizens expected to be solved.

The typical response was progressive disillusionment with the government, which became discontent with the state. It must be remembered that prior to independence there was very little attempt to create a positive sense of primary political loyalty to the state. In multinational states (which comprised the vast majority), public loyalty was more clearly identified with nationality, whether it be ethnically, historically, or tribally defined. When disillusionment began, the tendency was to blame other national groups and retreat to one's own group. (This is a phenomenon not only of the old Third World; to a significant degree, a similar process is occurring in the successor states of the Soviet Union and in the Balkans, notably the Yugoslav states.) When religion and other sources of division were added to the mix, its volatility could only increase.

Two other factors added to the crisis. One of the first institutions (in some cases the only one) to undergo modernization after independence was typically the military. In most cases this was not a reflection of some demonstrable need for self-defense against external enemies. Rather, new governments desired a military force as a symbol of strength and modernity, as a kind of national icon that proclaimed the new state was real. At the same time, the developed states were generally more than willing to provide military assistance as a relatively cheap means to curry influence.

As people like Morris Janowitz pointed out more than thirty years ago, developing-world militaries became a volatile part of the political landscape. Militaries by their very nature thrive on order and despise disorder, and as failing governments fell into increasing disarray, militaries viewed the process with growing dismay. To them, the problems tended to be matters of competence and efficiency (rather than more political problems like the absence or shortage of resources). Many military officers in the new states were trained or schooled in the West and considered themselves—rightly in many instances—the most competent elements within the polity. It is not surprising that some of them concluded they were the answer to the problem and seized power. The resulting spate of coups was especially—but by no means universally—noticeable in Africa where, at one point in the 1970s, nineteen of thirty-five black African countries were ruled by military juntas. (The phenomenon of officers trained in the West returning to overthrow their governments became so widespread that in the 1970s the school that had produced the most heads of state in the Third World was the U.S. Army's Command and General Staff College at Ft. Leavenworth, Kansas, earning it the nickname "coup college.")

The second factor was the intrusion of Cold War concerns. Military governments by and large proved to be little better (and in some cases worse) than the civilian governments they replaced, because the problems turned out to be political rather than administrative. Thus, in some cases the military, whose political skills were less developed than those of the leaders they replaced, became repressive (particularly of their opponents). Where the military was dominated by one ethnic, tribal, or national group, repression was often directed at other, similarly defined groups within the territory of the state (the relationship between the Hausa-Fulani–dominated military of Nigeria and other tribally defined groups, notably the Ibos, being a dramatic and continuing case in point).

The result of military domination and repression in a number of countries was the formation of opposition groups that, when subjected to further suppression, formed insurgencies to try to wrest power from the military. Military governments, in turn, were generally violently anticommunist (especially when their leadership had been educated in the West), and insurgencies thus turned for assistance to the communist states—the Soviet Union or China. China offered the Maoist strategy and ideology, and the Soviets, operating under the principles of the war of national liberation, offered ideological and practical advice, as well as a source of more worldly support, such as weapons. Thus, the Cold War managed to intrude on the dynamics of internal instability as well. In the 1980s the United States entered the competition for supporting insurgents through the so-called Reagan Doctrine, which declared it to be American policy to support movements whose purpose it was to overturn communist dictatorships. The policy was implemented in Nicaragua and Afghanistan.

Legitimacy and Authority. The dynamics I have been discussing can be thought of as a *crisis of authority and legitimacy.* The *World Book Dictionary* defines authority in a satisfactory, consensual way as "the power to command obedience; right to control, command, or make decisions; jurisdiction." In a purely political context authority is the right and ability to govern, in the sense of being able to enforce the rules of the political system on the citizenry.

Authority can have two bases: legitimacy and coercion. Legitimacy refers to the condition in which the people freely and willingly confer the right to govern to the state. Such conferral is based on a shared set of values and beliefs about how and who should govern, and the expectation that the outcome of the political process will be fair and acceptable.

The key element in conferring legitimacy to the the political system is a shared set of values upon which the population (or at least a high percentage of it) agrees. When that consensus is lacking, as is often the case in multinational states in which different nationalities hold different values and politics becomes a struggle by groups to impose their values on those holding different values, the result is often instability and the potential for violence.

In situations in which there is a lack of legitimacy because of the absence of shared values, the basis of authority is necessarily the imposition of authority, or coercion. It is a more unstable solution, because it means one or more groups is enforcing an order the basis for which parts of the population deem unfair or unjust, and to which they would not subscribe in the absence of coercive control. Politics under these circumstances becomes a struggle between competing groups, often describable as nations, to wrest control from one another. In the worst of situations, the struggle becomes violent.

This condition can better be understood in terms of a matrix, depicted in Figure 2.1.

Figure 2.1
Strong and Weak Societies and States

		State	
		Strong	Weak
Society	Strong	Cell 1	Cell 2
	Weak	Cell 3	Cell 4

I have introduced some new ideas here, notably those of weakness and strength as applied to the ideas of the state and society. For these purposes (and admitting the usages are not altogether conventional), a strong state refers to a situation in which the state's coercive capabilities and mechanisms are particularly robust, whereas a weak state has a less developed coercive component. By contrast, a strong society refers to a condition in which there is broad general consensus on the underlying values of the society, and weakness reflects a progressive absence of such agreement.

When placed in combination, these two factors can be used to describe the crisis of legitimacy and authority currently being experienced in many Second Tier states. Cell 1 of the matrix refers to a condition in which the state has strong coercive powers but in which there is also a strong consensus on underlying social values. In Western thought, this would seem to be an anomalous situation, because the existence of consensus should accompany the conferral of legitimacy and hence the absence of the need for a high level of coercion. This combination could exist where there is a "popular dictatorship" or at least the agreement that society's needs include the strict enforcement of the political order, as in Singapore (a condition some attribute to Eastern societies generally).

Cell 2 represents the Western norm, the general condition of the First Tier. In this combination, there is underlying agreement on social, political, and economic issues: the virtue of political democracy and market economy, which produce the freedom and motivation that nurture a quality economy. That support, in turn, means that the state does not require great coercive capacity, because it need only suppress criminal activity and deviation from the order. Ironically, the most advanced states that fall into this category also possess the most sophisticated technologies, allowing the greatest surveillance of their citizenry and hence the potential for the greatest coercive control. This fact is a matter of great contention within the political process and associated with one or another form of libertarianism.

Cells 3 and 4 represent the more problematic combinations and the situations in Second Tier countries most likely to result in instability and violence. Cell 3 represents the combination of a weak social structure and a coercive state, a condition most frequently associated with authoritarian regimes wherever they exist. Of concern here is not the ideological basis for a coercive regime (although it often was in the Cold War), but rather the need for a strongly coercive regime that can impose authority in the absence of a population that willingly accepts the authority of the state (in other words, confers legitimacy to the regime). In these circumstances, the absence of shared values means that some groups are imposing their values on others. The result, in some cases, will be resistance by those who feel they are oppressed. Resistance can become armed and violent; this describes the underpinnings of many insurgencies during the Cold War, as well as some post–Cold War violence such as Islamic fundamentalist actions in such places as Algeria and Tajikistan.

Cell 4 represents the final alternative, a situation in which there is an absence of both social cohesion and a strong governmental mechanism capable of imposing order on society. In this case, the result is likely to be a power struggle among groups at its rawest and most explosive, where there is little or no governmental ability either to mediate disputes peacefully or to suppress outbreaks of violence among groups within the state. The worst case is a failure of the state to function, and the term "failed state" is most obviously applicable in this combination of conditions. Contemporary examples of such a condition include Somalia, Rwanda, and Bosnia and Herzegovina. As a more generalized phenomenon, the potential for anarchical, failed states seems to exist wherever a coercive state collapses and is replaced by a weak state in which there is little underlying sense of common societal values. The most obvious examples include the successor states to the Soviet Union and the Balkans, where the potential for chaos is strongest, and the condition could also apply to such diverse places as India and China in the future.

The conditions described in Cell 4 are certainly not unique to the post–Cold War world, but they are more obvious today than during the Cold War. Certainly, the breakdown of old states and their violent reconstitution is not unique to the present day or to the current Second Tier. Western Europe, for instance, experienced a similar process during the nineteenth century. Periodic violent revolutions (in 1830 and 1848 and in the Paris Commune, for example) fought to establish national boundaries and political forms, accompanied by the weakening of absolute monarchism. The United States had to let considerable blood to determine the basis of its social order between 1861 and 1865. The Cold War, likewise, witnessed the removal of coercive constraints in the form of European colonial rule and the consequent struggle for political power within multinational states.

Figure 2.1 also suggests a kind of political development. Although it is admittedly Western in its emphasis and hence vulnerable to criticism on cultural terms, it suggests that the development of legitimate bases for societies is the key to developing strong, stable societies in which the political contest can be conducted nonviolently. This is another way of saying that the critical problem facing states in which violence is occurring is *state building,* where the key element is devising a series of agreements on the social basis of the state around which consensus can be built. This, of course, is a difficult process; it is at least arguable that the ability of outside mediation to create such conditions is questionable at best.

The Post–Cold War Pattern

Although one can easily overestimate the degree of difference between the Cold War pattern of internal violence and the contemporary pattern, I believe there are discernible differences, some of which have their roots in the Cold War and some of which are the result of its disappearance. It is not so much that a fundamental divide has occurred in the underlying political conditions that result in internal violence, but rather a change in emphasis. The pattern is tipping away from the more prevalent Cell 3 basis for internal war (strong, coercive states masking weak societies) to the Cell 4 basis (weak, failed states revealing weak societies). Reconstituting (or constituting in the first place) stability in Cell 4 circumstances is considerably more difficult than in Cell 3 conditions; this is a cautionary note for those who would be activist in mediating internal wars.

There are, I think, several dynamics at work here. One has to do with the wave of democratization that has been a part of the breakdown of the communist world and has extended beyond the boundaries of the old Second World. For the most part, the results of what Samuel P. Huntington has called the "third wave" of democratization have been positive. The spread of free elections to encompass all of the states of the Western Hemisphere except Cuba (much ballyhooed at the Miami summit of the Americas in 1994) certainly has contributed to a more tranquil, even upbeat Latin America than was the case ten or even five years ago. Democratic governments in a number of the former Warsaw Pact countries have enlivened the process in Poland and Hungary and facilitated the peaceful separation of Czechoslovakia into the Czech Republic and Slovakia.

The granting of the right to political freedom of expression that is at the heart of democratization has had a darker side, however. As the coercive cloak has been lifted in a number of formerly communist countries, freedom of expression has become the vehicle for the extremism of calls to national self-determination that are wrapped in an exclusionary form of nationalism often expressing itself in violence.

Woodrow Wilson (as the twentieth-century apostle of self-determination) would not have recognized the potential incompatibility between democracy and national self-determination. Yet such incompatibility exists—especially in places where ethnic and other hatreds had long been officially suppressed but never extinguished in the hearts and minds of populations. In these cases, the right to political expression has become the call for national separation, a situation that can "result in more ethnic homogeneity and less pluralism, meaning that they [separatist movements] often lack the deeper sociological foundations of democracy" such as growing tolerance and intergroup interaction, according to sociologist Amitai Etzioni. He adds that "excessive self-determination works against democratization and threatens democracy in countries that have already attained it."

This process has been most obvious in the former Soviet Union and Yugoslavia (which is not coincidental, given that Josip Broz Tito consciously designed Yugoslavia politically and demographically on the Stalinist model). The idea was supposed to be that, through an

Orwellian process of indoctrination and political socialization, there would emerge something often referred to as "Soviet man (or woman)," a breed of people so acculturated and conditioned that they would no longer think of themselves as Lithuanians or Tatars, but instead as Soviet citizens.

It has not worked out that way. Freed of the coercive control that marked them as Cell 3 cases, the older loyalties came bubbling forth with amazing speed and strength. The three Baltic states led the parade of secessions from the Soviet Union, reconstituting the fifteen socialist republics (provinces) into fifteen fully sovereign states by the end of 1991.

The process did not stop there. As old national loyalties resurfaced, there were increased cries *within* the newly independent states for further fractionalization, including anti-Russian sentiments against Russian ministries in the republics. The Abkhazians tried to secede from Georgia and form an Abkhazian state (and are still in de facto control of much Abkhazian territory), the Armenians fought to gain control of an Armenian enclave within Azerbaijan (Nagorno-Karabakh), and the Azeris countered by trying to reunite an Azerbaijani enclave cut off from the country by an Armenian corridor (Nakichevan). The government of Moldova raised the prospect of isolating their Russian and Ukrainian minorities (and possibly uniting with their ethnic brothers, the Romanians), until the Russian and Ukrainian governments informed them that such action would not be tolerated. More recent is the continuing bloody and embarrassing attempted secession of the Chechen Republic from Russia. When added to other forms of conflict such as Islamic fundamentalism in Tajikistan, the southern areas of the old Soviet state offer a rich and varied potential for mischief and violence that could parallel the horror of Bosnia and Herzegovina (the most ethnically mixed state in the former state of Yugoslavia). The potential for Serbian action in Kosovo should the largely Albanian population of that province seek unification with Albania provides another ugly prospect.

This phenomenon raises the conceptual problem of whether political freedom expressed as national self-determination entails the right to secession as well. Most scholars would agree with the assessment of Max Kampelman (former U.S. arms control negotiator) that it does not, but rather "that the right of self-determination of peoples does not include the right of secession. These are two separate rights." At the same time, there is the question of whether further balkanization of the globe is politically desirable in light of the unification of the global economy. Moreover, the reversion of peoples to older forms of loyalty like nationality, ethnicity, or even religion can only drive deeper wedges between people within regions and states, thereby exacerbating existing conflicts.

The end of the Cold War has contributed to the new pattern of internal war in at least two ways. The collapse of communist authoritarianism has moved some states of the old communist world from Cell 3 toward Cell 4, rather than toward Cell 2 (weak state, strong society); others remain in Cell 3, although without the official designation of communist states. At the same time, the end of the Cold War has eliminated competition for influence in the old Third World as First Tier countries abandon their interest in and control over Second Tier countries.

The Fate of the Second World. The outcome of the transformation of the old Second World into its post–Cold War forms remains problematic. Democracy seems to be taking hold in a few countries—notably the northern states of the old Warsaw Pact (Poland, Hungary, the Czech Republic) and Slovenia—allowing the possibility of movement toward Cell 2 and even the First Tier. The return of a number of former communists to power via the ballot box provides a note of caution about the difficulty of transition and the holdover appeal of the extensive social safety net constructed under communist rule.

A number of old Second World states remain rather clearly within Cell 3. States such as Ukraine, Belarus, and Kazakhstan can be described as moving toward democracy only if one adopts the most generous definition of democratization. In fact, much of the old communist nomenklatura remains in charge of governmental bureaucracies; old state-owned industries (with all their inefficiencies) have not undergone transformation, and many political leaders of the communist era remain in power, even if they rarely call themselves communists.

So far there has been relatively little movement toward full Cell 4 status in the old Soviet bloc (including the Balkans, which were not entirely within the Soviet orbit). Sections of the most unstable areas, the southern rim of the old Soviet Union itself and the former Yugoslavia, remain vulnerable to descent into the failed state category. A strong case can be made that this has already occurred in Bosnia and Herzegovina, where the land grab by Serbs and Croats in that most diverse of former Yugoslav states will not be fully resolved for some time, despite any internationally sanctioned accords. The crazy quilt of boundaries (almost all artificial and virtually impossible to defend militarily without outside assistance) that the settlement created and the deep animosities that have been revived among the principal groups in the region make it difficult to project a positive future for the state of Bosnia after the Implementation Force (IFOR) leaves. Within the former Soviet Union, the communal violence in Tajikistan has the greatest short-term prospects for creating a Cell 4 condition, but other states, such as Georgia, are also at risk.

The prospects for internal, and even occasionally international, violence remain great and can be organized around three basic concerns. The first is the potential for internal violence within the newly independent successor states, a problem that has already manifested itself and may well continue to do so. The non-Russian areas of Russia (mostly east of the Ural mountains) have a tentative commitment to Russia at best; it is likely that the Russians moved as brutally as they have in Chechnya at least partly to send a message to various other potential secessionists in the Russian Republic. The fact that the proposed Russian route for a pipeline to transport Azerbaijani oil to Western markets transverses the Chechen Republic was undoubtedly a major factor in the Chechen case.

The second concern is that internal strife will be directed at or will involve Russian minorities in the successor states. As part of the Stalinist pattern of "russification" of the Soviet Union, there are sizable enclaves of ethnic Russians in most of the successor states who are varyingly welcome among the ethnic and/or national majorities. In parts of the Baltics these enclaves have already been the victims of post-Soviet discrimination such as property and voting rights, and discrimination was threatened in Moldova. Russian involvement in Georgia (technically as part of a Commonwealth of Independent States—CIS—force) to stifle Abkhazian separatists was partially justified as protecting Russian nationals in the affected regions; Kazakhstan, among others, has a very large Russian population.

This population could come under threat in one of two ways. On the one hand, it could become involved directly, in the form of exclusionary nationalist attempts to purify states by "ethnically cleansing" the Russian population. In most cases this is not terribly likely, because such action would certainly trigger decisive Russian military response that, if not exactly championed by the international community, probably would not be strongly opposed either. On the other hand, Russians could be caught more or less inadvertently in the middle of internal (or international) conflicts within the region, a situation that would raise questions about what Russia should or might do to protect other Russians living in the near abroad.

The third concern is the appropriate international response in the event of internal conflicts in the territory of the former Soviet Union. The Russians have important interests in any such conflicts because of the likely entanglement of Russian nationals in such conflicts. At the same time, any Russian activism is likely to be construed as imperial by those it would oppose, and by parts of the international community as well.

There are three possible patterns that international efforts might take, and each has been implemented in different parts of the successor states. The first pattern is the use of CIS forces as peacekeepers. The CIS is the putative security successor to the Soviet Union that is supposed to coordinate the mutual security concerns of the successor states. Although it is widely viewed as little more than a front for the Russians and does not have the universal membership of the successor states (the three Baltic states do not belong), the CIS can act as a legitimating forum for Russian and Ukrainian "peacekeeping forces" in Moldova, according to official UN documents (*Peacekeeping and International Relations,* January/February 1994) cited by Project Ploughshares.

The second pattern is cooperation between the UN and the CIS. In the case of the Abkhazian separatist war in Georgia, there is a UN Observer Mission in Georgia (UNOMIG) that came into being in August 1993, consisting of 126 observers from 22 countries—including two Americans—at the end of 1994. (For a summary of the operation, see *United Nations Peace-Keeping: Update, December 1994,* pp. 160–171.) This small observers group was reinforced by CIS peacekeepers. The third pattern is to appoint a strictly UN presence, such as the small (initially forty-member) United Nations Mission of Observers in Tajikistan (UNMOT) in December 1994.

The isolated and relatively low-key nature of these problems has not forced a decisive action by Russia or anyone else. But what will happen if there is a truly serious internal or interstate conflict in the former Soviet Union? The most likely point of conflict is Azerbaijan, either because of an extension of the war with Armenia over Nagorno-Karabakh and Nakichevan or internal violence (possibly Islamic fundamentalist) within Azerbaijan. Either possibility is potentially important to the system because Azerbaijan's acknowledged claims to the oil and natural-gas fields adjacent to and under the Caspian Sea (the world's largest remaining known, untapped reserves) provide an important alternative to continued reliance on the Persian Gulf. Negotiations are underway to exploit those reserves and bring them to market. Violence that might interrupt the ability to exploit those reserves would be of great importance to the major powers of the First Tier (making Azerbaijan one of the only places in the Second Tier, other than the Persian Gulf, that engages strong First Tier interests).

Effects of the End of the Cold War. The other visible way in which the end of the Cold War has affected the post–Cold War political pattern of internal violence in the Second Tier is the gradual withdrawal of the superpowers from much of the Second Tier. This has left a vacuum of interest that may have decreased the degree of leverage the major powers have over the conduct of individuals and groups within Second Tier countries.

Cold War competition in much of the Second Tier was always somewhat artificial and contrived. Neither the United States nor the Soviet Union had many intrinsic interests in most Second Tier regions, unless a particular region contained strategically important mineral or other deposits (the southern part of Africa, for instance) that might be denied or made more difficult to obtain by the opponent, or a strategically important geographical feature such as a naval choke point (the Straits of Malacca or Hormuz), the closure of which could create problems for an adversary in times of crisis or war. But such interests were derivative of the competition rather than directly important to either side.

Although the old Third World was not of critical importance to either Cold War opponent, it did become part of the general competition for loyalty, influence, and prestige. Because the problems of the developing world were not readily translatable into terms of communism-anticommunism, few Third World states had much interest in comprehensive commitment to one side or the other in the competition (a case such as Egypt between 1956 and 1973 being an exception). Rather, their primary interest was in attracting economic and military assistance to aid their development, and they gradually realized their best strategy was to play one Cold War side off against the other. The exception was the rise of an insurgency, in which case the besieged government would choose one Cold War opponent (usually the United States, at least until the Reagan doctrine) and the insurgents the other (usually the Soviets or Chinese), and at least a tactical alliance would be forged.

As Daniel S. Papp pointed out in an extensive study published in the mid-1980s, this courtship of the developing world changed over time. Between 1945 and the middle 1960s, the United States pretty well controlled the playing field; the Soviets, partly out of a lack of resources and partly because Stalin thought the Third World unimportant, did not compete. When the United States became preoccupied with Vietnam between 1965 and 1975, the Soviets entered the competition, achieving something like equal influence by the end of the period. Reeling from the Vietnam war debacle, the United States withdrew temporarily from the active field of play between 1975 and 1980, during which time the Soviets gained influence in places like Angola and Mozambique. After 1980, the United States rejoined the competition.

By the middle 1980s, however, the Soviets—and notably the supporters of Mikhail Gorbachev—had concluded that this competition, which was yielding very modest advantages for the Soviet Union, was part of the ruinous effect of the continuing Cold War. Subsidizing the Cuban economy at the rate of about $5 billion a year, in addition to costly support for besieged governments (Afghanistan) and interminable insurgencies (Angola and Mozambique), became an albatross to a Soviet system desperate for capital and expertise for economic development to compete with the West. If the Soviet Union (or its successor, Russia) was to have a chance, the Cold War competition had to be abandoned. Under Gorbachev the Soviet Union began its withdrawal from the Second Tier; under Boris Yeltsin Russia's withdrawal is virtually complete.

The result is a vacuum. Soviet/Russian retreat has left the United States with little reason to remain engaged in most Second Tier areas. Lacking intrinsic interests or the derivative interest in countering Soviet influence, there was not much reason for continued U.S. involvement. Withdrawal of an active American presence could thus be thought of as part of a "peace dividend" whereby resources formerly committed to the competition could now be devoted to other purposes, such as the reduction of the U.S. deficit. This tendency was only reinforced when the 1994 congressional elections swept into office a Republican majority. The new House leadership featured a Contract with America whose primary aim was to reduce federal spending, including U.S. Second Tier spending.

The removal of the artificial Cold War patina from relations between the major powers and the Second Tier is not altogether unwelcome, in that it allows a refocusing of those relations on the real problems associated with economic and political development should the First Tier decide to involve itself at all. On the other hand, the result may be further to marginalize the concerns of the Second Tier: The geopolitical consequences of providing economic assistance have been dramatically reduced, and the instances of violence, including internal violence, have moved outside of the areas of concern.

Violence Between 1991 and 1993. The problem, in other words, may be that the willingness and ability to influence and moderate the conduct of internal war may have been reduced by the end of the

Cold War. The spate of activity by the UN in the period immediately following the Cold War suggested a much more activist stance. According to the UN's own statistics (as of December 1994), the world body had authorized a total of thirty-five peacekeeping or observation missions during its history. Eighteen of those had come into existence between 1948, when the UN Truce Supervisory Organization (UNTSO) was placed between Israel and Jordan, and the end of 1990. That means that seventeen additional missions were formed in the four-year period between 1991 and 1994 (none were instituted in 1995). Of these, five were authorized in 1991 (in Kuwait to monitor the ceasefire, Angola, El Salvador, Western Sahara, and Cambodia), four in 1992 (Croatia and Bosnia, Cambodia, Somalia, and Mozambique), six in 1993 (Somalia II, Uganda-Rwanda, Georgia, Liberia, Haiti, and Rwanda), and two in 1994 (the Aouzou Strip in Chad and Tajikistan). Seventeen of these thirty-five missions remained in place at the end of 1994, five commissioned prior to 1991 and twelve since then. Moreover, almost all were put in place after conflicts had occurred rather than to prevent or ameliorate conflicts.

It is reasonably clear that the three-year period between 1991 and 1993 represented an aberration in the level of UN activity, and that UN-led missions will decrease in the immediate future. This is not to say that the UN will not have a legitimating role in authorizing essentially unilateral actions (the United States in Haiti, Russia through CIS in Georgia) or even group actions (deputizing NATO to enforce the peace agreement in Bosnia). Rather, it is to suggest that the UN may no longer be the "agency of choice" for deciding whether or how to respond to Second Tier violence.

I think there are several reasons for this. The first is overreach by the UN. The resources available to the world body are decidedly scarce, and to carry the ambitious agenda Boutros-Ghali suggested in *An Agenda for Peace* and elsewhere requires large voluntary contributions or assessments that the members are proving reluctant to provide. One major reason for this reluctance is the UN's track record: It has proven itself impotent in Bosnia for an extended period of time (for reasons examined at length in Chapter 6), it could not broker a stable settlement in Somalia, and it failed utterly to prevent or minimize the carnage in Rwanda. A growing part of the publics in the major First Tier democracies that would be expected to provide many of the resources for systemic actions have concluded they are uninterested in the task, do not believe the UN is up to solving the problems, and do not think these problems important enough to demand their serious attention or action.

There is also a small but growing sense that there may not be a lot that anyone can do to change the emerging pattern of violence. This line of reasoning suggests that the spate of Second Tier violence occurring in the lower rungs of the developable subtier may simply be part of a natural process of development through which all or most societies pass, and that to interfere would likely be futile.

The bottom line is that the end of the Cold War has been accompanied by an apparently reduced willingness and ability to control internal violence in the Second Tier. Governments and potential insurgents no longer have ideological patrons who provide them with the wherewithal to commit violence and then expect some influence over how that violence is carried out. The motivation to place restraints on client behavior may well have been entirely selfish—to avoid being embarrassed by the actions of a client or because high levels of barbarity might risk confrontation. Although acts of barbarity occurred among the clients of the superpowers in such places as Mozambique, they were more the exception than the rule.

A third part of the new pattern of internal Second Tier violence is its appearance to the attentive world. This factor is the result of the introduction of global television as the principal way publics (and for that matter, elites) are made aware of the terrible things happening around the world. Television's omnipresent eye was not as much a part of the mix before the end of the 1980s, when advances in telecommunications technology such as very light, mobile video camcorders and satellite transmission of photographed images made it possible to cover almost anything to which a reporter could gain access. We now know more about the pattern of violence (and virtually everything else) than we used to and possibly more than we want to. It is difficult to assess whether the Cold War pattern would contrast so clearly with the current pattern had it been subject to modern levels of scrutiny.

The Role of the Media. There is not yet strong evidence about whether global television is an agenda setter that influences what the public perceives (as many critical of the media would have it), or whether it has a more passive influence, reflecting rather than shaping reality (as most media people would prefer to think of it). The first major post–Cold War crisis in which global television was an apparent factor was the Persian Gulf War and its aftermath. The war itself, and especially the air campaign that preceded the liberation of Kuwait on the ground, was a media event of precision-guided munitions chasing Iraqi soldiers through bunker doors and down air conditioning vents. The campaign began for television, with the first bombs raining on Baghdad just before the end of the evening television news programs on January 16, 1991. CNN alone estimates that nearly two billion people watched their coverage of the war worldwide at one time or another.

The aftermath of the war demonstrated even more dramatically the potential power of television. One of the major effects of the way the war ended was to leave Saddam Hussein's regime with much of its power, including its helicopter gunships, largely intact. In the wake of the war, Hussein trained those forces on his traditional internal enemies, notably the Kurds of Iraq's northeast who had supported attempts to overthrow him during the war. Mindful of attacks on their villages by Hussein's forces in 1987, many Kurds fled their villages and headed toward what they hoped would be safe haven in Turkey and Iran. On the bleak mountainsides of southern Turkey, CNN found the refugees suffering and dying; so did President George Bush, an avid CNN watcher.

Bush and other American and world leaders were appalled by the images they saw and determined to "do something" about the suffering and carnage. The result was a relief effort, called Operation Provide Comfort, to save and eventually return the Kurds to their homes in those parts of Iraq they think of as Kurdistan. The United States, France, and Great Britain guaranteed the Kurds safety from the Iraqi government by creating an exclusion zone *within Iraq* in which the Iraqi government is banned from operating. A similar arrangement, Operation Southern Watch, was declared to protect rebellious Shiites in southern Iraq in 1992. Both remain open-ended commitments. The point is that neither operation likely would have occurred had it not been for the voracious eye of global television. The plight of the Kurds was, by all measure, horrible and inhumane; it was also not the first time such a disaster had occurred in the world (or, for that matter, to the Kurds). What was different about Kurdish suffering, in contrast to the suffering of millions elsewhere, was that it was on television for everyone to see.

A similar phenomenon occurred in late 1992, when television discovered the politically motivated starvation of hundreds of thousands in Somalia. The images of rail-thin Somali children with bloated bellies and large, sunken eyes captured public sympathy worldwide. Something had to be done, and the response, officially commissioned by the UN, was swift. Accompanied by somewhat sheepish Navy SEALS (whose clandestine arrival onto the beach was leaked to reporters, who were waiting with full lighting as they clambered out of the water), the Marines arrived, securing Mogadishu and beginning to reestablish the food-distribution system.

The public was initially enchanted by this Operation Restore

Hope. The landing occurred about three weeks before Christmas of 1992, and television screens were filled with images of American Marines teaching Christmas carols to apparently eager Somali children. Never mind that the children were Muslims for whom "Silent Night" had little appeal (the candy bars they received doubtless had much more meaning); we Americans were reaching out and helping the needy; we were, in the phrase Bill Clinton used to justify sending troops to Bosnia, doing "the right thing."

The problem, which should have been obvious at the beginning but only became so with painful experience, was that solving the food shortage only addressed the symptom of Somalia's underlying malaise. Starvation was partly the result of a long drought that was beginning to break, but mostly the result of a political struggle between Somalia's major clans for control of the political system following the deposition of dictator Siad Barre in 1991. Starving rival clans had become a major part of that struggle; bags of grain were the weapons of choice in this chaotic war.

Inevitably, the UN, including the Americans who were the major participants in the effort, became entangled in the anarchic struggle. In the early days Mogadishu clan leader Mohamed Farah Aidid attempted to court American support for his claim to power, in which he was unsuccessful. When the Americans withdrew and then returned with the mandate to disarm the fighters in Mogadishu, Aidid became the enemy and fought back. The deadly, unsuccessful 1993 American Ranger raid against a Mogadishu hotel in which Aidid was supposedly conducting a meeting (which turned out to be an ambush), and the subsequent image of the corpse of an American serviceman being dragged through the dusty streets of Mogadishu, epitomized the futility of trying to end the chaos.

The lesson of Somalia, not unlike that of Vietnam, is clearly "no more Somalias." To conclude from this lesson that the United States (or the UN, or anyone else) should abandon all involvement in Second Tier conflict may be extreme. But if First Tier countries learn to more thoroughly assess the actual structure of problems in Second Tier countries before they act, and to determine their real interests (where there are any) *and* whether their intervention is relevant to solving the problems that actually exist, then "no more Somalias" is not a bad lesson to learn at all.

The final part of the new pattern is the apparent absence, or at least reduction, of more conventional forms of conflict. It is central to the current thesis that Cell 4 conflicts, occurring within the politically least-developed states (the failed states), now occupy a more central position in the landscape of violence primarily because more conventional conflicts, both international and internal, have become somewhat less prominent. There has not been a major cross-border war since Iraq invaded Kuwait in 1990 (the sporadic fighting between Ecuador and Peru over disputed Amazonian territory notwithstanding), and virtually all the Cell 3 conflicts that remain unresolved have their roots in the structure of the Cold War.

It has also been argued, by Steven Metz among others, that internal wars have not really changed much at all. Metz argues, for instance, that the motives underlying internal war (individuals and groups disliking or even hating one another), at least from the vantage point of the fighters, have changed only to the extent that leaders no longer justify their actions in communist-anticommunist terms to get assistance for their causes. Constraints may be slightly reduced, but the only real change is that, in the "fire sale" of excess weapons no longer needed for the Cold War, there has been an inflow of additional and more sophisticated weapons than were formerly available.

I would take at least partial exception to this construction. Whereas the motives for individuals and leaders may remain the same in places like Bosnia (which is close to a Cell 3 conflict in which motives are conventional), protecting drug dealers or looting the countryside are not the traditional motives that groups calling themselves "liberation armies" have used to justify or, particularly, to guide their actions. If one is to understand or thwart violence, one has to understand what motivates and hence what can change behavior. The continued intransigence and unwillingness to negotiate a peace on the part of the Tamil Tigers in Sri Lanka cannot be entirely understood without realizing that there is an Indian murder warrant out for the group's leader that would almost certainly be served if he agreed to peace.

One need not make the extravagant claim that the new internal war is sui generis, a form so fundamentally different from that of the Cold War as to render knowledge of that pattern obsolete. Nor do I argue, as some have done, that the new pattern represents a change in the extent or the orderliness of conflict. There were many internal squabbles within the Cold War system, some of which made more sense than others, and the same is true today. What is different is that some forms now appear less frequently, making the remainder seem more prominent.

I do argue that, particularly at the level of motives, the root causes of at least some internal wars are different than they were during the Cold War and that these differences require us to modify the way we approach their solution. It is not enough, for instance, to apply counterinsurgency doctrine developed to blunt the Maoist mobile-guerrilla strategy to the ongoing narco-insurgencies in Peru and Colombia. Nor is it clear that traditional views of centers of gravity and battles for the hearts and minds of men help explain the Rwandan rampage or the criminal insurgency in Sierre Leone. The Cold War formulations of insurgency and counterinsurgency require modification and, more important, those modifications will likely result in a much more cautionary approach to outside involvement in those kinds of conflicts.

THE ECONOMIC DIMENSION OF CHANGE

The classic literature on internal war, an extension of the general literature on political development, suggests a pattern of economic change that either facilitates or impedes the emergence of internal conflict. That literature in essence argued that the countries most vulnerable to internal conflict were those that were experiencing some level of economic development but were not yet to the point of development that results in stability.

One need not dwell in great detail on these arguments, although they do affect the way we have traditionally thought about the causes and cures of internal war. Rather, I will briefly summarize the way we understood the economic dimension of change and violence that emerged in the Cold War period and see how well it seems to apply to the post–Cold War world of tiers.

The Cold War Pattern

An analysis of the economic impact on internal violence and stability inevitably becomes entangled in the broad dynamics of decolonization. The countries emerging from colonial domination were not only politically ill-prepared for self-rule; they were also almost universally poorer than they had been during the colonial experience, and often their economies, in addition to being underdeveloped, were skewed toward serving the purposes of the colonial ruler. The vast majority, in other words, had yet to enter the first industrial revolution (as described in Chapter 1); their economies remained heavily dominated by subsistence agriculture, natural-resource extraction, and possibly a bit of cottage industry (the characteristics of the developable subtier of the Second Tier).

This condition gave rise to two parallel concerns within academic and policy domains, each of which has some bearing on the present discussion. One concern was the justice of the condition in which colonial rulers left their former colonies when they granted independence. This debate was, as noted earlier, heavily influenced by the pro-Marxist *dependencia* theorists, who argued the injustice of a situation in which the colonial rulers had artificially stunted the growth of Third World economies. This situation created the squalid conditions so prevalent in the Third World and, more important, created a need and an obligation on the part of the former colonists to aid in the economic development of the newly independent world, presumably to promote standards of living equivalent to those of the most developed countries.

The moral merits of this concern do not have direct relevance to the pattern of violence in the system. Here the second concern of those interested in the development of the formerly colonized world enters the picture. Decolonization universally produced both the desire for economic development and the inability to meet the economic expectations that newly free people had. The result was a spate of discontent that manifested itself in a wave of internal wars in the then Third World. Part of the explanation for this situation lay in the nature of the developmental process.

A number of scholars observed the phenomenon and tried to understand it. W. W. Rostow was the first to give it a name: the "revolution of rising expectations." James C. Davies referred to a "J-curve" effect, and Ted Robert Gurr to a phenomenon he called "relative deprivation." All shared a common conceptual core, which is depicted in Figure 2.2.

The basic idea is that traditional societies (the kinds of very static, underdeveloped societies that predated colonial rule) go through a developmental process from their traditional situation to one of development (in the modern sense, First Tier or developed Second Tier). During the process of development, however, there is a period of discontent during which societies are prone to political instability and even to violence.

The basis of this discontent, as depicted in the figure, is the divergence of people's expectations of society, especially in terms of economic well-being, from the performance of that society in meeting those wants. When this "want-get" ratio becomes the widest, then the potential for discontent is the greatest.

This process is not unique to the current Second Tier. The same process occurred in Europe during the eighteenth and nineteenth centuries (it can be thought of as an underlying theme of much of Charles Dickens's depiction of England) and in the United States in

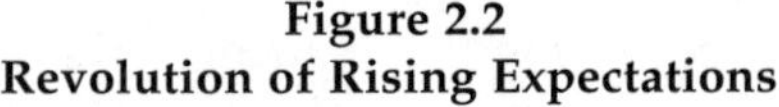

Figure 2.2
Revolution of Rising Expectations

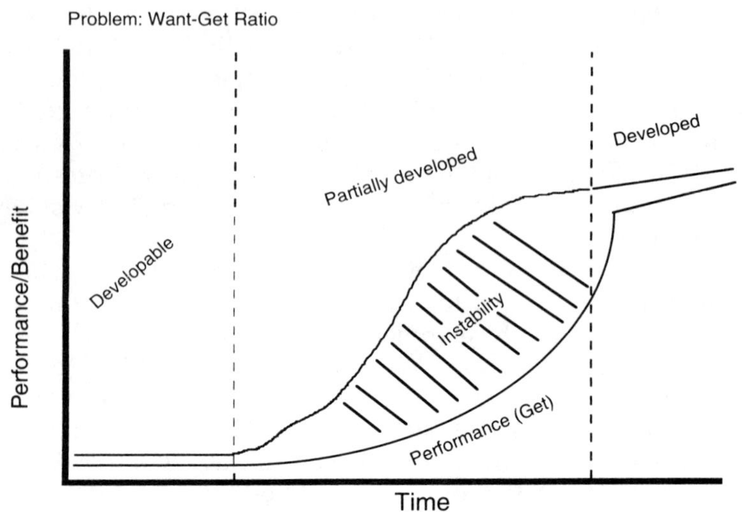

the period between the end of the Civil War and the end of the nineteenth century.

What triggers instability is not the existence of deprivation—traditional societies were quite stable politically—but the recognition of deprivation and the realization that it need not continue. This is the core of Gurr's relative deprivation: the recognition that deprivation is not universal, that the basis of deprivation is either unfair or incapable of rectification within the system, and, most important, that there is the possibility of change through political action. When societies, or groups within societies, see that their deprivation relative to others' has these characteristics, then political activity, including internal war to overthrow those creating the injustice, becomes a possibility.

This thesis can be applied to the developmental subtiers of the Second Tier, as the figure shows. Within traditional, developmental-subtier states, the performance of society is deficient but people's expectations are low. Generally speaking, the people are physically isolated, without perspective on the nonuniversality of their misery, and lacking ideas about political change; the likelihood that they will rise up against their government is minimal. At the other end of the spectrum, once development has been achieved (First Tier or developed Second Tier), the ability to satisfy the desires of the vast majority is achieved, and the motivation to violence decreases.

The violence-prone period occurs when development has begun (the partially developed subtier of the Second Tier status). For a broad variety of reasons (such as enforced savings to encourage further development; corruption or incompetence on the part of political leaders; or lack of patience with the pace of change), it is during this period that people are most likely to become discontented with their conditions. When they do, alternative political leaders will arise with the promise to create positive change. Inevitably, one possible way to achieve reform, especially if the government will not voluntarily relinquish power, is the use of violence.

Cold War concerns enter at this point, in two ways. First, part of the context of the Cold War was the economic competition between the command, socialized economies of the communist world and the capitalist and mixed economies of the noncommunist world. Although in retrospect the intellectual aspects of that competition seem ludicrous (given the abject failure of socialism as an economic system), at the time the weaknesses of controlled economies were not so widely known, and communism did offer a set of concrete guidelines about how to transform an economy into a "socialist utopia," for which the West had no alternative.

Second, the communist world offered material as well as conceptual succor for those seeking basic change in economies with Western structures (to the extent the economies had structures at all). Economic discontent could thus serve as the triggering mechanism to engage the Cold War competition, in some cases nonviolently, in other cases violently.

The Cold War depiction of internal war was deeply influenced by the idea of economic development as the cause of underlying instability and hence violence. In turn, that concern prompted a debate about the efficacy of assisting societies through the developmental process as quickly as possible so as to minimize the period of time during which they were vulnerable to destabilization. Foreign economic assistance, for instance, was sometimes advocated on the basis that it would shore up support for regimes supported by the West (by helping those regimes narrow the want-get gap) and thus make them more impermeable to communist influence.

This contention was never entirely accepted nor laid to rest during the Cold War period, and it remains a matter of conjecture and disagreement in the post–Cold War world. Is instability and the vulnerability to internal violence simply a natural part of the development of societies, as inevitable as puberty and adolescence are to humans? If so, is there much that can—or for that matter should—be done to try to intervene in these processes, or should they simply be allowed to follow their natural course, regardless of how disagreeable that course may be?

The Post–Cold War Pattern

Without adopting the apocalyptic and untenable position that the economic factor in internal war has changed so fundamentally that there has been a sea change in how economic conditions affect the likelihood and form of internal violence, one must acknowledge that there has been a change in the kinds of states in which internal violence is occurring. That change affects how we view internal war in two ways. First, the concentration has moved away from the developing countries to those that have not yet entered the developmental process, and the variety and concentration of motives underlying internal violence have changed as well. Second, and as a result of those changes, old solutions based in stimulating development are not so obviously appropriate (nor as affordable from public sources).

Twenty-five of the thirty-eight internal wars ongoing in 1993 involved states in the developable subtier of the Second Tier. This represents about two-thirds of a category that includes about half of the countries of the Second Tier. Moreover, these countries are located outside the general growth areas of the global economy as judged by participation in the various existing and proposed regional organizations: NAFTA and the proposed Free Trade Area of the Americas, APEC, and the EU. Violence in the poorest countries is not a post–Cold War phenomenon: Rwanda and Burundi, for instance, experienced their share of ethnic violence in the past, and the general carnage that marked Liberian politics from the late 1980s until the middle 1990s occurred in poor countries during the Cold War. What seems to be different is that *more* of the violence appears to be occurring in these kinds of places.

This is not what the development literature of the 1950s and 1960s told us to expect. Instead of occurring in countries where, by objective standards, the stakes are not very high at all, violence is supposed to accompany the developmental effort as groups become aware of economic disparities and act to rectify that situation, by violence if necessary.

Why does the pattern appear to have changed? I would suggest two contributory factors that are subtle modifications of the Cold

War expectations. The first is the *impact of global media.* In orthodox theories about gaps between people's expectations and their aspirations, it was generally assumed (at least implicitly) that some fruits of the developmental process would become apparent and be obviously unfairly allocated, thereby triggering a sense of relative deprivation. In a television age in which no part of the globe is too remote to receive images that graphically depict the difference between those who have and those who do not, the stimulus of developmental activity is no longer so necessary as a trigger. Just as it was argued that the widespread distribution of battery-powered portable radios in the 1950s and 1960s began the process of ending the isolation of large parts of the Third World (notably Africa), television may be freeing the activation of relative deprivation from its economic, developmental mooring.

The second factor I would suggest is the *absence of ideological encouragement for traditional insurgencies.* It is no surprise, after all, that most of the insurgencies in developing Third World countries had some ideological connection to the communist-anticommunist competition, in which notably the Soviet Union or China (or both in competition) could offer the theoretical justification, the strategic and tactical instruction, and the physical wherewithal for a successful fight against an unjust government. For the ambitious, there was a trip to Moscow and a course at Patrice Lumumba University to provide the basis for insurgency.

That basis for insurgent organization has disappeared. As the Soviet Union began its descent into what became its implosion, one of its first acts was to cut its connections (especially economic) to "wars of national liberation." Nikita Khrushchev had proclaimed such support to be a cornerstone of Soviet policy in the 1960s, and that policy contributed to Soviet bankruptcy. There are only a handful of insurgent groups that still pretend to be communist (the Khmer Rouge of Cambodia and Shining Path of Peru, for instance), but they are hardly movements on the ascendancy, and new Marxist insurgencies have not arisen.

The ideology of the post–Cold War world, particularly as it applies in the partially developing countries, is political democratization and market-based economy. Not all countries in that category will achieve either or both, but the key to greater prosperity lies in moving, and being perceived to be moving, in that direction. Joining the majority, rather than engaging in guerrilla warfare in steamy jungles, appears to be the wave of the present.

The dual facts that new internal war tends to occur in the least developed countries and that ideological justification has waned are reflected in the apparent change in the causes of these wars (in some cases the term *war* seems oddly inappropriate). During the Cold War the majority of wars were fought by insurgents seeking to overthrow and replace a government in power, normally with some degree of economic justification. This purpose helped to structure the violence and the means by which it was undertaken, and in turn to structure responses to that violence. In a number of post–Cold War instances (even if they have some roots in the Cold War period), the ideological element is almost completely missing.

The two most obvious nonideological formats that have emerged are the *criminal insurgencies* (of which the drug-based narco-insurgency is a prominent example) and the *ethnic insurgencies.* The Liberians created the prototype of the criminal insurgency, the purpose of which appears to be to destabilize parts of the country by forcing the removal of government authority, and then to terrorize the population as a preface to engaging in criminal activity (robbery, extortion, rape, and the like). This is a form that spread to Sierre Leone and may have attractions in other places in central Africa as well. The narco-insurgency variant, currently in vogue in South America (notably Peru and Colombia, but budding in Bolivia), involves either an alliance of mutual economic convenience and profit (Peru) or an economic merger (Colombia) between narcotics traffickers and putative insurgents. The purpose of the alliance is to disrupt governmental ability to operate effectively in contested areas. This form of insurgency has potential in southeastern Asia (Burma/Myanmar, for instance) and in parts of the former Soviet Union historically engaged in the opium/heroin trade. Ethnically based conflicts have, of course, been among the most publicized, especially those in Bosnia and Rwanda. The closest thing we can find to an ideological base is a call for Islamic purity by fundamentalist movements.

What is notable about these kinds of conflicts is that they are neither neatly explained by nor combatible with strategies honed for Cold War–based insurgencies in which the purpose was to gain control of government in order to provide some economic benefits. The criminal insurgents, including the narco-insurgents, have *their own* economic gain as their motive, not some ennobling societal goal to which an appeal can be made. Ethnic violence may be waged for political gain (keeping anti-Tutsi Hutus in power had something to do with incitement of the Rwandan slaughter), but its purposes are hardly ever ideological in the sense of offering an alternative, and presumably superior, form of governance.

As some (Metz, for instance) have argued, the absence of some lofty goal may or may not affect the motivations of the foot soldiers, who may act because they hate or fear their neighbor or even because they are bored by their civilian lives. The differences may, however, be important for considering the leaderships of these kinds of movements: What actions or appeals will cause the narco-insurgent or the ethnic zealot to lay down his or her arms?

One very real question is whether appeals to development, a staple in the process of understanding and containing internal violence in the Cold War, have relevance in these situations. The justification for development (beyond its altruistic motives) was always dual (if interconnected): moving target states through the developmental process, the end of which was stability, and counteracting communist encroachment and appeal. The connection between the two was that stable, developed societies would be less vulnerable to communism than states in the throes of development.

It is not at all clear that this rationale applies to the newer forms of internal war, in which economic improvement or some form of ideological basis (with an economic content) is absent. The poorer countries of the developable subtier are not attractive to private investors, for reasons of infrastructure defect but also certainly of internal violence, and there is far less public developmental assistance available from the First Tier. The developmental paradigm, in other words, may simply not be relevant to the new form of internal war.

CONCLUSIONS: POLITICAL AND ECONOMIC FACTORS IN NEW INTERNAL WAR

In this chapter I have attempted to provide a comparison between the political and economic bases of internal war during the Cold War and in the post–Cold War world. No claim has been made that either period is so unique that none of the violence in the Cold War period is present in the post–Cold War environment, nor that the forms of internal violence emphasized today were unknown during the Cold War. Rather, the argument is that there have been discernible shifts in the emphasis of different forms, and that the reasons for these shifts have roots in political and economic change.

In summary, the process of decolonization, overlaid by Cold War considerations, produced political dynamics whereby internal violence was largely structured and rationalized in terms of organized insurgencies the purpose of which was to replace one government (usually anticommunist) with another (usually at least nominally Marxist). At least part of the dynamic was a political appeal by both sides for the loyalty of the population. The bulk of these conflicts arose in situations in which there was a weak society (absence of consensual values) but where the coercive power of the state was considerable (strong state). This, of course, described Cell 3 states in the state-society matrix. The criterion of success was whether the insurgents could overcome that coercive capability.

In the post–Cold War world that pattern has changed. With the withering of ideological difference and the movement toward greater freedom of expression, a concomitant change has been the weakening of coercive ability in a number of places. When the weakening of coercive authority occurs in a country in which there is little social cohesion, the result can be a "failed state" (Cell 4: weak state, weak society) vulnerable to attack from a variety of quarters, including criminal insurgencies that have no traditional political goals. Economically, the old paradigm that internal violence occurs mainly in states undergoing development has apparently given way to a tendency of internal violence to occur in the poorer states.

If the paradigm for the old problem of internal war does not quite fit the new pattern, do the old solutions apply? It is possible that the apparent movement from partially developed to developable states represents no more than a kind of natural evolution, that the removal of constraints and new stimuli like global television have simply catapulted these states into the same point in the developmental cycle that has been reached in other parts of the world throughout history, in which case there may be little that can or should be done to interrupt the cycle.

There will, however, be reactions whenever these kinds of conflicts break out, due at least to the publicity of their horror. One possible reaction will be to suggest that intervention be undertaken on humanitarian or other grounds. The track record of such action is uncertain: The system failed entirely in Rwanda and almost entirely in Bosnia, and the long-term effect of the civic-action response by the United States in Haiti has yet to unfold (although the ability to effect a peaceful succession to President Jean-Baptiste Aristide will further its chances of success).

Given that there will be the temptation for the United States (and others) to engage in "peace operations," "operations other than war," or some other euphemism for intervention in new internal wars in the future, it is necessary to examine the structure and dynamics of more traditional insurgencies and counterinsurgencies, to contrast these with new internal wars, and to determine the efficacy of outside interference in insurgency-counterinsurgency situations. This will be the focus of the next three chapters.

REFERENCES

Clausewitz, Carl von. *On War.* Princeton, N.J.: Princeton University Press, 1976.

Davies, James C., ed. *When Men Revolt and Why.* New York: The Free Press, 1971.

Etzioni, Amatai. "The Evils of Self-Determination." *Foreign Policy* 89 (Winter 1992/93): 21–35.

Gurr, Ted Robert. *Why Men Rebel.* Princeton, N.J.: Princeton University Press, 1973.

Huntington, Samuel P. *The Third Wave: Democratization in the Late Twentieth Century.* Norman, Okla.: University of Oklahoma Press, 1991.

Janowitz, Morris. *The Military in the Political Development of the New Nations.* Chicago, Ill.: University of Chicago Press, 1964.

Kampelman, Max M. "Secession and the Right of Self-Determination: An Urgent Need to Harmonize Principle with Pragmatism." *Washington Quarterly* 16, 3 (Summer 1993): 5–12.

Mao tse-Tung. *The Collected Works of Mao tse-Tung.* Beijing: Foreign Language Press, 1957.

Metz, Steven. *America in the Third World: The Future of Counterinsurgency.* Carlisle Barracks, Penn.: Strategic Studies Institute, 1995.

Orwell, George. *Burmese Days: A Novel.* London: Secker and Warburg, 1986.

Papp, Daniel S. *Soviet Policies Toward the Developing World During the 1980s: The Dilemmas of Power and Presence.* Maxwell AFB, Ala.: Air University Press, 1986.

Project Ploushshares. *Armed Conflicts Report: Causes, Conflicting Parties, Negotiations, 1993.* Waterloo, Ont.: Institute of Peace and Conflict Studies, 1994.

Rostow, W. W. *The United States in the World Arena.* New York: Harper and Row, 1960.

Snow, Donald M. *Distant Thunder: Third World Conflict and the New International Order.* New York: St. Martin's Press, 1993.

United Nations. *United Nations Peace-Keeping: Update, December 1994.* New York: United Nations, 1995.

3

Contrasting Shapes of Internal War

Although the frequency of internal war, generally described in terms of insurgency and counterinsurgency was often overshadowed by the greater concern with managing the Cold War military competition, it was the most common form of warfare during the period between the end of World War II and the end of the Cold War. The process typically began with movements to remove colonial rule, and when some postindependence governments failed to satisfy all or parts of their populations, the response was sometimes an insurgency for the purpose of forcefully toppling the government. In some cases a military coup d'état might itself spawn further insurgent activity.

The pattern of insurgent warfare during the Cold War developed a certain level of predictability that allowed for a reasonable understanding of internal-war situations. Based upon that understanding, it was possible to predict the likelihood of success of outside interference in internal processes. Although there was a relatively small pre-Vietnam War literature on the nature and conduct of insurgency, much of the academic and the bulk of the professional-military literature on the subject came with the assessment of that particular debacle.

We can identify two aspects common to these insurgent wars. The first is that insurgent warfare became a part of the Cold War competition itself, the proxy ground in which the communist and noncommunist worlds could compete through their various clients without the great risk of face-to-face confrontation. Throughout the Cold War this meant that the West usually found itself assisting besieged governments that were at least purportedly anticommunist, while the Soviets and Chinese sponsored insurgencies at least willing to adopt some of the language of Marxist revolutionism in return for the material and other support necessary to sustain their military efforts. That pattern began to change in the 1980s. Although the United States had earlier run covert actions against noncooperative governments, Ronald Reagan pronounced that it would be American policy to support anticommunist insurgencies seeking to overthrow communist regimes. This so-called Reagan Doctrine was applied most prominently in Nicaragua and Afghanistan. In renouncing the Brezhnev Doctrine (which asserted the right of the Soviet Union to come to the aid of besieged communist governments), Mikhail Gorbachev (in *Perestroika*) also condemned more broadly outside interference in internal affairs: "Every nation is entitled to choose its own way of development, to dispose of its fate, its territory, and its human and natural resources." Sponsorship also created some leverage for the sponsors over the nature and conduct of hostilities.

The other aspect common to these wars was the way in which insurgent warfare was fought. Most of the insurgencies, and certainly the overwhelming number of analyses of insurgency, counterinsurgency, and outside intervention into insurgencies, are based on the Maoist strategy of mobile-guerrilla warfare. This strategy, evolved and perfected by Mao Zedong in his successful campaigns against the Japanese occupiers and the Nationalist Chinese, provided the broad conceptual base for the war in Vietnam and for numerous other insurgencies—particularly those with some Marxist attachments—during the Cold War.

Because Mao had studied Clausewitz's *On War,* his themes and prescriptions had a heavily Clausewitzian influence and content. The set of military instructions that form the mobile-guerrilla strategy is associated with a communist and generally treated as coterminous with the political persuasion of its author. But the connection is more coincidental than it is causal: Groups have used variants on the strategy for a very long time. At the same time, the articulated strategy, when followed faithfully by its purveyors, presents a considerable number of difficult problems for those who would counter insurgency. The track record of counterinsurgency, and especially outside intervention on the side of counterinsurgents, does not initially inspire much enthusiasm for the prospects of success.

Internal war remains the dominant form that warfare takes in the post–Cold War world. The great regional conflicts of the Cold War—the Arab-Israeli and Indo-Pakistani confrontations, for instance—have moved rapidly toward resolution or become essentially dormant. The problem of the Indian subcontinent in particular has moved much more toward internal divisions that have spawned separatist movements such as those of the Tamil Tigers of Sri Lanka and the Kashmiris in India. What essentially remains is a series of internal conflicts, some carrying over from the Cold War, others emerging in its wake.

Some observers have argued that the removal of Cold War structures and strictures has produced a more unruly, more dangerous world. The threatened spread of nuclear and other weapons of mass destruction is often cited as evidence of this new danger and Iraq and North Korea as great symbols of that threat.

In my view this assessment is incorrect. If messy internal wars that do not fit into neat patterns or categories are the form of violence, that does not mean they are any more numerous or any more destabilizing to the international system than they were before. The reason they now show up to public view is that they are the only form that violence currently takes. The concern for weapons proliferation has existed for thirty-five years and has only gained prominence now in the absence of the greater concern of avoiding World War III. The fact that national-security problems have become restricted to internal wars in areas of limited interest and even more limited escalatory potential, represents a considerable improvement in the security condition. The current environment is certainly less dangerous than that of the Cold War, when the threat of general nuclear war that could end civilization as we know it was the central concern with which we dealt.

If the problem of new internal war is less pressing and even less important than Cold War problems, neither is it inconsequential or unworthy of study and understanding. New internal war (and the continuation of "old" internal war from the Cold War period) remains a phenomenon that is persistently public—thanks largely to global television—and is the greatest barrier to the creation of global tranquillity. Moreover, from a military standpoint there is almost a vested interest in understanding and responding to this form of warfare, given that it is virtually the only kind for which military forces (at least American) are likely to be called upon in the foreseeable future.

The fact that these wars are sometimes genocidal gives them an important moral aspect as well. Situations that are prone to insurgency-like conflicts are unlikely to disappear, especially in those parts of the world excluded from the global economy. Their dynamics are likely to be analyzed in terms of insurgency theory as it was developed during the Cold War. The question is whether that theory, including our understanding of counterinsurgency and outside intervention, is adequate to describe and prescribe policy alternatives to deal with the current problems.

This chapter will address that question by examining traditional insurgency theory and the problem of counterinsurgency, including the problems associated with outside intervention on the side of counterinsurgents. Throughout the discussion I will suggest ways in which some of the new internal wars may not conform to the traditional patterns and constructs.

INSURGENCY AND THE APPEAL OF POOR MAN'S WAR

The form of warfare we now call insurgency probably dates to the first time one armed group confronted another of apparently superior strength and took evasive action for self-preservation and to try to blunt the advantage that superior force provides. The contemporary development is often traced to Sun Tzu's *The Art of War,* a military manual prepared over 3,000 years ago to aid in conducting China's dynastic wars. This work was apparently the basis for much of Maoist thought (see *The Collected Works*), which, in turn provided much of the inspiration for Vietnam's Vo Nguyen Giap, Che Guevara in Bolivia, and other post–World War II adherents. Applications of one variant or another tailored to particular locales have appeared in places as diverse as El Salvador and Mozambique.

Insurgent warfare has an appeal well beyond the narrow bounds of the Cold War experience. A good bit of the more effective fighting in the American Revolution can be attributed to the actions of people like Francis (the "Swamp Fox") Marion, Nathaniel Gates, and the Green Mountain Boys, all of whom used tactics (mostly learned from fighting the Indians) of which Mao would have approved. The Chechens in 1995 adopted similar tactics in the face of massive assaults by the Russian Army.

Insurgent warfare is a unique breed of fighting, the purpose of which is to negate the advantages of a militarily superior opponent. This "poor man's war" had particular appeal for Third World groups seeking to overthrow governments that were, at the outset, considerably stronger militarily, because it offered a geopolitical blueprint by which an initially inferior force can, by virtue of its patient application of that force, gradually turn the tables and prevail.

Insurgency Defined

There is little agreement on what exactly insurgency is or on what terminology should be used in its description. The terminological tangle may be the worst: What I will call insurgency is also referred to in different sources as guerrilla war, unconventional war, uncomfortable war, low-intensity conflict (LIC), and civil war, among other names. Each of these descriptions offers a slightly different emphasis on the phenomenon at hand. They all describe a form of warfare that has a distinct political basis and military style, which I will use cumulatively to describe the phenomenon of insurgency.

The political element of the definition is that insurgencies are *civil wars* in the normal sense of that term: *organized armed violence between groups within a state for the purpose of overthrowing and replacing an existing regime or to secede from an existing state.* This suggests that insurgencies are at heart wars of total political purpose, where both (or in some cases all) combatants have the common purpose of seizing governmental power. Totality is achieved because the insurgency must overthrow the existing regime to achieve power, and the government cannot succeed until it crushes the rebellion against it. This generally requires capturing or killing the insurgent leadership—or discrediting it to the point that it loses support and leaves. An insurgency is quintessentially a political contest, in which military action may facilitate a resolution of the struggle for authority and legitimacy, but in which that struggle remains the central contention. The definition is also heavily Clausewitzian in its conscious subjugation of military activity to the political purposes the violence promotes.

The second element of insurgency is that, at a military level, it is conducted as *unconventional warfare.* This means that insurgencies are normally conducted, at least by the insurgents, *employing other than traditional European strategies, tactics, and means of organization.* Typically this means organization as guerrillas—small bands of irregular, part-time soldiers who may or may not wear identifiable military uniforms and who engage in hit-and-run tactics such as ambushes or acts of terror. The purpose of this military format, which has its roots in Sun Tzu, is to avoid large-scale direct clashes with main units of a conventionally organized government force, which generally would be organized along classic European lines and have superior firepower.

The two aspects of insurgency can thus be combined to provide a comprehensive definition of insurgency: *unconventional warfare waged for the purpose of overthrowing an existing regime or seceding from an existing state.* The political objective of insurgencies is thus conventional and Clausewitzian: the conduct of the politics of gaining power by means of armed violence. Insurgencies differ from more standard forms of warfare in the means by which they are conducted, and from other forms of internal violence in their explicitly political purposes.

The U.S. Army's Field Manual (FM) 100-20 (1989 edition) generally agrees with this definition, producing a series of "elements common" to insurgencies. The goal of insurgencies, it asserts, is to "replace the government's legitimacy with its own," implying that part of the task is indeed the political conversion of the populace. It seeks that conversion by appealing to the population with "a program that explains what is wrong with society and justifies its actions." Insurgency, in other words, is politics by other means.

It has been argued recently that this definition may be inadequate to describe certain contemporary internal wars that are considered non-Clausewitzian. The alliance between so-called insurgents and drug lords in Colombia is difficult to tie to any articulated program aimed at gaining political control of the government; rather, its apparent purpose is to deny the government the ability to assert its control in certain parts of the country so as to protect the drug industry's operations. The criminal insurgency in Sierre Leone similarly has had no stated program at all and, if it is interested in seizing political power, it has yet to say so. This is part of the way in which these new wars are non-Clausewitzian.

This criticism is correct in a sense: Such conflicts as those in Colombia and Sierre Leone are not cases of insurgency as defined here. However, this does not mean that the definition of insurgency is defective, but rather that these outbreaks of violence are something other than insurgency. Different language and different concepts are needed, therefore, to describe and understand the phenomenon. That is, of course, the central concern of this book.

Insurgency Described

In order to make detailed comparisons between conventional insurgencies and contemporary forms of internal violence, it is necessary to describe the principal characteristics of conventional insurgencies. The first relates to the goals of the insurgents and of the government they seek to overthrow. The goals of the two parties are similar in that both seek the same end—physical control of the government—but different in the military requirements necessary for their attainment. For an insurgent band to reach its goal it must gradually shift the balance of power away from the government's initial monopoly of force to its own. This requires a patient, long-term program of gradual conversion and sapping of government strength. Along the way, however, the insurgency remains vital and can calculate progress by its ability to avoid destruction by government forces; thus the insurgency "wins by not losing."

Progress for the government is more exacting. If the insurgency can progress, and even win in the long run by avoiding military defeat, the government can only win by successfully defeating the insurgents: breaking their military forces and capturing or dispersing their leadership. The government, in other words, has to "win to win" in the sense of needing militarily to destroy the insurgency, while the insurgency is alive and a problem for the government as long as it avoids destruction. This creates a kind of asymmetry of objectives between the two sides, which makes the government's task more daunting.

The symmetrical political goals of insurgents and the government means that insurgent wars are wars of total political purpose: the absolute objective of capturing or retaining control of the political system. Such absolute goals are rarely amenable to peaceful or negotiated settlement: typically, someone wins and someone loses. Because losing may result in personally extreme consequences (such as death), compromise is unlikely. The limited exception is a situation wherein neither side can assert itself and exhaustion overwhelms both (or all) parties, as was the case in El Salvador in 1992 and may prove to be the greatest hope for lasting peace in Bosnia. This is an important observation for the contemporary scene, because it suggests that there may be internal wars that are not amenable to international intervention, either to negotiate a settlement or physically to claw apart the antagonists. In such cases the only solution may be to allow the contending parties to fight it out until there is no more fight left in them. Somalia may be a perfect example of this dynamic.

The second characteristic of conventional insurgencies is the struggle over centers of gravity, when both sides attempt to appeal to the same population. This affects and moderates the military conduct of insurgency as both a political and a military quest. What differentiates conventional insurgency is that the political element is much more central to the relative calculus than is the case in conventional international wars. In wars between states, political objectives may dictate military strategies and objectives, but they rarely intrude at lower levels. American soldiers in World War II, for instance, did not worry that actions they took against Japanese forces might alienate those forces or the Japanese population. The objective, after all, was to defeat those forces and impose unconditional surrender on the Japanese.

The battle for what Lyndon B. Johnson first termed "the hearts and minds of men" is crucial to both sides in conventional insurgency. Ultimately, the side that is most successful in its political appeal is most likely to prevail, because the people support that side and reject the other. Part of that appeal may be negative—selective terrorism to keep population segments in line, for instance—but part must be positive, aimed at convincing the population that its interests would be better served by one side than the other.

The need to appeal to the same center of gravity is much more important, both politically and militarily, to insurgency than to standard interstate war. Any military action may have serious political consequences that can increase either support or opposition for the side that carries it out. The loyalty of the population is the ultimate prize, but the potential support for both sides resides *in the same population.* The practical problem becomes how to attack the other side's support base without attacking one's own or alienating the uncommitted. The manipulation of public opinion can become a major part of the tactics of war; for example, an insurgent band may dress in government uniforms and commit some atrocity that it blames on the government. In the classic dilemma from the Vietnam War, the government would conduct civic work, perhaps building schools, during the day that would then be occupied by the insurgents at night. Knowing this, should the government bombard those structures at night that it built during the day? The tactical decisions are not easy to make.

One important effect of the common need to make a positive appeal to the general population is to moderate the conduct of violence. Terrorism or atrocity may occasionally seem necessary, but it is unlikely to be an effective long-term or general practice. Committing large-scale acts of atrocity may temporarily cow a segment of the population into passivity; it will almost certainly not lead to political conversion unless the other side acts even more atrociously. Knowing that particular acts of violence may do more political harm than military good moderates how and against whom acts of violence occur.

This moderating element of traditional insurgency apparently contrasts with the characteristics of the new internal war. One of the most striking aspects of the rampage in Rwanda or the purposeful starvation in Somalia is the level and even wantonness of brutality against civilian populations. The dynamic of mutual centers of gravity seems to be missing from these "wars." There is no sense of physical restraint on the violence because there is absolutely no interest or concern about conversion and support from target populations. These are not wars for the hearts and minds of men, but naked attempts by one group to subjugate or destroy another; these new internal wars are not insurgencies at all. The calculation of the political consequences of military actions on target populations is much more akin to that of interstate wars, in which such concerns are decidedly secondary if they exist at all.

The third characteristic of conventional insurgencies concerns the manner in which they are conducted. At the outset of insurgencies, when movements are forming and developing their physical base, the government typically has the overwhelming monopoly on force. (During the Cold War this was due mostly to the largesse of the major powers.) For an insurgency to avoid extinction and then gradually to shift the balance of power toward itself required adoption of a strategic game plan. In conventional insurgencies the most generally adopted plan was some variation of the Maoist mobile-guerrilla warfare strategy.

Mobile-Guerrilla Strategy

The insurgent strategy associated with Mao Zedong evolved during his campaigns of the 1920s, 1930s, and 1940s against Chiang kai-Shek's Nationalist Chinese and Japanese invaders. It is a political and military plan. The purpose of the strategy is gradually to shift power from a government to the insurgent group through a combination of political and military actions that ultimately will win the sympathy of a country's population away from the government and toward the insurgent cause. It has been applied successfully, in one variant or another, in some countries (such as Vietnam) and unsuccessfully in others (such as by Che Guevara in Bolivia).

The strategy consists of three distinct stages, as shown in Table 3.1.

Table 3.1 Stages of Mobile-Guerrilla Warfare

Stage	Goal	Emphasis
Organizational	Survival, infrastructure	Political: battle for popular support
Guerrilla	Shift in balance of power	Political and military: attrition
Final	Overthrow of government	Military: destroy government forces

The names for the stages are my own. Others use different names to describe the same dynamic; General Giap, for example, uses the term contention for organization, equilibrium for guerrilla, and general counteroffensive for final.

There are five important characteristics of the strategy. First, its stages are sequential: An insurgent group practicing the strategy begins at the organizational stage, moves through the emphasis on guerrilla fighting, and conducts final operations. Second, the strategy is evolutionary: There are not sharp breaks in action so much as gradual changes in emphasis, such as between guerrilla and conventional fighting. Third, the stages are eclectic: There are no rigid timetables attached to its conduct, but rather a general understanding that, for instance, at some point the movement will gain sufficient force to begin to challenge government forces in guerrilla ambushes, and that at another point the balance of power will have shifted enough to allow a general confrontation. Fourth, the stages are reversible: If, for instance, the battlefield conditions change once the insurgency has entered the climactic final stage, the insurgents can simply revert to guerrilla warfare and wait for more favorable conditions. Fifth, the stages require considerable patience on the part of insurgents: Premature commitment to movement between stages may result in utter disaster for the insurgents. This partly explains the fate of Che Guevara in Bolivia, where he elected to skip the first stage altogether, hoping the outbreak of violence would cause a support base to emerge (the so-called *foco* principle).

In the first stage—organizational—insurgency is the idea of a usually fairly small group that is discontented and has decided that only the violent overthrow of the government can accomplish its political goals. Because the insurgency is small and weak at this point, it is most vulnerable to destruction by the capture and suppression of its leadership cadre. The problem is that the group may be so small and obscure as to avoid the attentive eye of the government's police or paramilitary apparatus.

Weakness thus defines the insurgency's problem in the first stage and creates two imperatives: physical survival (avoidance of capture) and development of a political program on which to base and then to broaden its appeal. These imperatives dictate strategy in the first stage. The first task is to find a sanctuary, a safe place that, by virtue of support for the cause (or alienation from the government), will provide protection for the insurgents as they organize and begin to broaden the support base. Preferably, the sanctuary will be established within the country, indicating some level of support for the movement; a sanctuary outside the country indicates either a powerful government suppressive capacity, or the general lack of support for the insurgents. (The failure of insurgents over time to establish an internal sanctuary, as in the case of the Nicaraguan contras during the 1980s, is a rather clear sign that the insurgency has insufficient support to succeed.)

Once the sanctuary is established the insurgency can begin the process of growth. According to Maoist method it does this by establishing itself as the government in the sheltered area and providing superior services and relations than those of the government. It is axiomatic that the government must be less than exemplary for an insurgency to form in the first place. There may be a need to suppress government supporters through negative acts (a primary role of the revolutionary militias during the American Revolution). The balance between negative and positive acts toward the population is itself a fairly accurate gauge of real support for the insurgents: Shining Path insurgents in Peru, for instance, rule the areas they control almost exclusively by terror, indicating the general regard in which they are held by the local population.

Reaching out to the population allows the insurgents to gain strength. Popular support can promise not only sanctuary but access to food, shelter, and the like. As its popularity increases, more and more people become willing to join the insurgent movement, so that it may begin to recruit the forces that will eventually fight the insurgency itself. Mao argued that two kinds of forces had to be organized and trained: guerrilla fighters who would conduct the second phase of operations, and a conventionally trained army that would be prepared for the final campaign to bring the government down.

Entering combat with government forces at this stage is generally to be avoided. The insurgency remains small and weak, it may not have sufficient access to arms through an outside patron (the recruitment of which Mao derided as unnecessary, but which was standard in Cold War insurgencies), and its forces are unlikely to be adequately prepared to confront government forces. In such circumstances, activities are concentrated on political acts of conversion, with perhaps an occasional attempt to lure the government into committing some politically damaging act.

When the insurgency decides its support base is sufficiently solid and its guerrilla forces sufficiently competitive, it enters into the second stage of guerrilla warfare. This is the critical stage of mobile-guerrilla strategy because it is the period in which the insurgency becomes gradually stronger and the government gradually weaker through a patient application of political and military strategy. It is also the phase in which a weaker insurgency demonstrates that it can overcome great odds relatively inexpensively, which is one of the reasons that insurgent war is sometimes referred to as "warfare on the cheap."

Like the first stage, the second stage has its own distinctive dictates. During this phase the insurgency introduces guerrilla warfare into its political actions (which continue and even expand as the insurgents seek to extend their appeal to greater parts of the population). The phase begins with the insurgency still at a deficit of actual available power, but through a careful campaign of attrition it will gradually shift the balance of power away from the government and toward itself.

Militarily, the emphasis is on guerrilla warfare: The guerrilla forces of the insurgency are activated but must carefully choose the times and points of encounter. Deficient in both manpower and firepower, the guerrillas must heed Sun Tzu's advice only to engage the enemy on its own terms: "When the enemy advances, we retreat; when the enemy pauses, we harass; when the enemy seeks to avoid battle, we attack; when the enemy retreats, we pursue."

The classic guerrilla tactic is the ambush. While avoiding the main body of enemy forces, the guerrillas try to locate small, isolated government units and lure them into traps. The guerrilla forces greatly outnumber government forces at this point of contact, and proceed to destroy those outnumbered troops. When government forces are superior to the guerrillas, on the other hand, the guerrilla units simply dissolve into the countryside, hiding away their arms and melting into the general population.

This style of fighting has several purposes. By fighting only on their own terms the guerrillas are overwhelmingly successful in combat, and gradually gain the reputation of winners, which is intended to aid recruitment of additional guerrilla and conventional fighters. At the same time, the morale of government forces is undercut: Whenever government forces take the field in search of guerrillas, they either find no guerrillas and return to barracks empty-handed, or run into an ambush and are defeated. As morale suffers, increasing numbers of government forces desert and leave their weapons behind them, or defect to the more successful guerrilla forces. The government is then forced into the involuntary conscription of increasingly reluctant new soldiers.

This dynamic gradually frustrates those who support the government and shifts the balance of power toward the insurgents. An insurgency that is faithful to the dual Maoist dictates of political persuasion and adherence to the principles of mobile-guerrilla warfare is extremely difficult to defeat if it reaches the second stage. If the insurgency does not progress, then probably one of three conditions has not been met. The insurgency may be failing to convert the population to its cause (to achieve legitimacy); heavy reliance on terror to coerce the population is a good indicator of this. It may not be faithful to its own strategy; a large number of pitched battles would be one indicator. Or it may be conducting its campaign in a physical environment detrimental to its chances of success, such as in a small country with highly developed communication and transportation networks that facilitate government pursuit.

If the insurgency is successful in the second stage, it enters the third and decisive stage, the purpose of which is to defeat the government forces and overthrow the government itself. Militarily, this calls for the activation of the conventional forces of the insurgency, assuming that the insurgents have been faithful to Maoist doctrine and have developed such forces, and that the government forces have been sufficiently weakened that insurgent forces can conduct successful direct assaults.

Experience has revealed certain signs that the third stage is being approached. A 1989 U.S. Army publication, *Guide to the Study of Insurgency*, provides a useful list. It includes the progressive withdrawal of domestic support for the government, critical population segments turning against the government, a growing popular perception of regime illegitimacy, a growing belief that the insurgents are the true nationalist heroes, and other opposition groups joining the insurgency. On the international level these are accompanied by the progressive withdrawal of foreign support for the government by former supporters and even allies, and growing support for the insurgents.

Such changes are reflected in the military situation. The government loses control over population and territory as the insurgents seize and control the countryside, leaving the government isolated in a few major cities between which it cannot safely communicate or traverse. Increasingly bold guerrilla and terrorist acts are carried out against government officials and supporters. The government is incapable of preventing such attacks, and the effort increasingly saps the economy, leaving goods and services in shorter supply and thereby further alienating the population. Most critically, the levers of coercive power are progressively lost as well. As failures multiply, there may be serious infighting within the government in the form of military plots or coups, troops may be diverted from fighting the insurgents to participation in political maneuverings (a particular problem in Vietnam in 1964 and 1965), and insufficient forces are available for the government to engage in effective counterinsurgency.

When the insurgents are sufficiently emboldened by their success and the government's failure, they enter the third stage. Guerrilla forces, which are useful for sapping government strength but incapable of confronting and defeating more heavily equipped, firepower-intensive conventional forces, give way to more conventionally configured forces for the final offensive. If the insurgents miscalculate their strength and enter this stage prematurely (or meet an unexpectedly strong opponent, as did the Viet Cong and their North Vietnamese allies in 1965, in the Ia Drang Valley), they can simply revert to the second stage and wait for a more propitious opportunity.

The Appeal of Insurgency

Although not all insurgencies attempting some form of the Maoist strategy are successful, there are enough instances of its success to give it appeal for groups in the appropriate circumstances. The success of Mao Zedong in the Chinese Civil War created a post–World War II appeal, but the success of the Vietnamese against both the government of the Republic of Vietnam and the armed forces of the most powerful state in the world, the United States, provides the evidence that poor man's war can indeed succeed.

For an insurgent group to maximize its prospects of success it must remain mindful of three basic concerns. The first is a recognition of and a consistent approach to its *center of gravity.* The importance of this idea cannot be overstated, because it largely distinguishes true insurgent warfare from other varieties of organized armed violence. The quest for the loyalty of the national population gives insurgent warfare its political nature; insurgents must be constantly aware that their political and especially their military actions will have direct consequences in the battle for that loyalty.

The second concern is a focus on the *political objective.* If all warfare in the modern state system is political in its purposes, insurgent warfare is even more so. The average guerrilla fighter or government soldier may not be motivated by lofty political principles; fear for his or her life, hatred of members of the opposition group, or the simple call for adventure in an otherwise unexciting existence may be motivation enough. At the strategic level, however, the leadership must subordinate military action to political control, with the realization that individual military acts can have politically positive and negative effects on the long-term achievement.

The third concern is the *measurement of success.* Unlike conventional warfare, wherein progress is measured by the movements of armies, the capture and control of territory, and the success of battles and campaigns, the progress of insurgencies is more clearly measured in terms of the progressive transfer of political loyalty from the government to the insurgents. Following the arrows of military campaigns on maps and color coding parts of the map as under government control have relatively little meaning until the climactic stages of insurgent war; during the guerrilla stage, after all, the insurgents simply melt away when large government army units approach. Moreover, a strategy of melting into the population and retreating in the face of superior force cannot have the possession of territory, beyond a sanctuary, as its objective. Standard measures of success do not apply until the very end. In China in 1949, for instance, the communists controlled over 90 percent of the country at the time of the final offensive, with the Kuomintang forces isolated in a handful of largely urban areas, at which point the standard measure *was* applicable. The same was true in Vietnam at the time of initial American intervention, when the Viet Cong were apparently entering the third stage.

Successful insurgents understand that their basic measure of success is their continued survival. As long as the insurgency persists, it remains a problem for the government, which can only succeed by crushing the insurgency entirely. Recognizing that insurgencies win by not losing requires considerable patience for the insurgents; conversely, measuring success is equally frustrating for those seeking to counter the insurgency.

The Future of Insurgency

Does insurgency, particularly in its traditional form, have a future? At the most obvious level it certainly appears so. The preconditions for insurgency—economic deprivation, political malfeasance, and illegitimacy—continue to abound, although possibly in more isolated areas and in fewer countries as the waves of democratization and the globalizing economy penetrate more places. Nonetheless, there remains no shortage of potential locales for violence aimed at replacing regimes.

What forms will such insurgencies take? One possibility is that there will be a continuation of the conventional pattern identified with the Cold War. To the extent that insurgency and communism were related, this is unlikely given the state of appeal of communist ideology; however, there is no necessary correlation between the strategy and any particular political worldview. It is possible that some form of insurgent warfare might be waged in the name of political democracy (a prospect that Rod Paschall propounds in his *LIC 2010*); a country such as Myanmar/Burma would seem a ripe candidate for a democratic insurgency, possibly with American assistance justified as a permutation of the Reagan Doctrine (assisting anti-authoritarian in addition to anticommunist movements). Some form of the strategy might also be adaptable to fundamentalist Islamic movements in places such as Tajikistan or Algeria. But it is not always clear that the political objective of Islamic activists/insurgents is as much to control the government as to influence whoever is in power to return the system and society to more orthodox Islamic values.

There are several variants of the new internal war to which the older pattern does not so obviously apply. These (mostly) post–Cold War examples can be differentiated from conventional insurgencies according to the following criteria: whether the "insurgent" movement had the overt purpose of gaining political power, the degree to which the parties pursued the political loyalty of an identical center of gravity, the degree (conversely) they relied on terror and intimidation rather than positive appeals, and the extent to which they followed something like the mobile-guerrilla strategy in waging war.

Somalia. The systematic starvation of one clan by another certainly had (and continues to have) an overtly political objective: for one clan leader to claim power over others. But there the comparison ends. There was no common, identifiable center of gravity toward which all sides sought to appeal. Rather, the withholding of food was essentially a terrorist tactic to force the members or followers of other clans to surrender; there was no attempt at positive political conversion. Moreover, there was little evidence of military strategy, tactics, or discipline. The predominant "military" image relayed was of the so-called technicals: teenagers darting about in roofless Toyota 4-by-4s brandishing mounted machine guns to terrify the citizenry.

Peru. The ongoing narco-insurgency and its emerging variant in Colombia offer another variant, although the two are somewhat different. The insurgency by Sendero Luminoso (Shining Path of the Communist Party of Peru, or SL) is a Cold War artifact, with its basis in the particularly extreme Maoist ideology propounded by its founder, Abimael Guzman. At least in its early phases, Shining Path embraced the mobile-guerrilla strategy and sought to wrest the political loyalty of the largely Indian population of Peru's interior from the government. As such, it began as a fairly orthodox insurgency, although its ideology was so extreme it could gain essentially no outside sponsorship. (It viewed even the practice of Maoism in China as a theoretical prostitution and sought to cleanse Maoism and establish a sort of fundamentalist variant.)

Essentially three things detached the Shining Path insurgency from its mobile-guerrilla moorings. The first was that its ideology proved to have little appeal to any sizable part of the population. It was thus forced increasingly to engage in brutal acts of terror to maintain control over the areas in which it operated (beheading reluctant supporters was a method of choice for political conversion of others who might share their reluctance). Only the fact that government forces were, until their reform by President Alberto Fujimori, often more brutal than Shining Path provided any basis for popular support.

The second factor was the open alliance between Shining Path and the *narcotraficantes* of Colombia, who swooped into the Upper Huallaga Valley of Peru in their small airplanes to obtain the coca leaves on which the cocaine industry relies. Shining Path's first dealing with the traffickers was to act as intermediary between them and the peasant coca farmers to reduce lawlessness and exact a fair price for the crop (in addition to protecting the growers from the Peruvian Army). Unfortunately, Shining Path became the protector of the traffickers as well, charging landing fees for their small planes in return for protection from drug enforcement efforts by the Peruvian and American governments. Shining Path has become dependent on these drug fees to finance its other activities.

The third factor was the capture and imprisonment for life of Guzman by Peruvian officials. Although many disputed the sagacity of his ideology, the movement owed what little coherence and direction it had to his leadership. No individual or group has effectively taken his place.

The Shining Path insurgency has been transformed by these experiences into something less than it was. In the absence of Guzman, plans to transform Peru into a Maoist paradise (which probably meant something like the "paradise" created by the Khmer Rouge in Cambodia between 1975 and 1978) are no more than a faded memory in which no one, probably including SL members, seriously believes. The movement maintains physical control of parts of the coca-growing region, but both it and the lawlessness it spawns are hated by the local population, and Shining Path can continue to rule only through the most brutal acts of terror. Nevertheless, the movement is likely to continue for some time as a politically pointless narco-insurgency.

Colombia. This "insurgency" is conducted by three groups that operate at one time or another: the Revolutionary Armed Forces of Colombia (FARC), the National Liberation Army (ELN), and the People's Liberation Army (EPL). Despite their impressive names, none of these groups has ever articulated any particular political ideology or made any serious effort to appeal for broad support among the population. Each remains in essence a criminal organization that hires itself out to the highest-bidding drug cartel to help shield its drug manufacturing and transportation activities. Terms such as strategy and center of gravity, which had some meaning for describing the original Shining Path, cannot be applied to these movements.

Sierre Leone. This criminal insurgency was inspired by a similar situation in Liberia. The "rebellion" has had no known spokesmen or political program; it does not seem to have the goal of gaining political power. It has no reason to appeal politically to the population in the areas in which it is active; its "strategy" is marauding terror of the subject population and denying control to the government so that the government cannot suppress its lawlessness. The fact that government forces have been known to act as atrociously as the rebels does not improve matters. Whether the recent return to civilian rule will improve the situation remains to be seen.

Rwanda. The campaign of genocide against the Tutsi minority and those Hutus who were sympathetic to the Tutsi (at least to the extent of opposing their systematic slaughter) was, at least apparently, politically motivated as part of an attempt to keep in power a conservative Hutu government. The conduct of hostilities, however, certainly was not a campaign aimed at the hearts and minds of those they opposed; the goal was the elimination of that portion of the population. There was no common center of gravity in Rwanda that could act as a restraint on the nature of the violence. Moreover, it is impossible to discern anything even vaguely suggesting a military strategy or set of articulated military goals.

These examples suggest that there is at least a subset of new internal wars that vary significantly from insurgency as understood prior to the end of the Cold War. They may be exceptions to a more general trend, just as Khmer Rouge action in Cambodia was an exception to the Cold War pattern. Nevertheless, it may be necessary to learn how to counter the new insurgency.

THE DIFFICULT PROBLEM OF COUNTERINSURGENCY

In many important ways, the problem of defeating an insurgency that has progressed beyond its vulnerable first stage is more difficult than the insurgents' task (unless the insurgents violate their own strategies and doctrines, which is always a possibility). Part of the difficulty is that the existence of an insurgency often is not recognized as a threat to the regime until the insurgents have entered the second stage of the mobile-guerrilla strategy, at which point they are difficult to defeat militarily and have probably developed enough of a political support base to make their eradication difficult.

The Dynamics of Counterinsurgency

Insurgencies rarely begin or succeed if the vast majority of the population has accorded legitimacy to the regime. The urge to rebel and the predilection to support an insurgency presupposes a degree of alienation between the regime and at least a part of the population. That alienation may stem from the corruption, despotism, or incompetence of the regime, its cronyism, and the maldistribution of resources; it may spring from the suppression of one or more groups by the government on an ethnic, religious, or other basis. Whatever the source, the existence of an insurgency, and especially one that has survived long enough to enter the second stage of activity, indicates that the battle for popular loyalty is at least in some jeopardy. The government must take this factor into account as part of its counterinsurgent strategy.

One may consider this a romantic depiction of insurgency: Not all insurgencies enter the second stage on a wave of popular appeal against a venal government. Shining Path's ideas of political conversion are decidedly draconian, even cutthroat, and their sway over those they putatively rule is based almost exclusively on terror. Does this not give the lie to romantic ideas about a compromised battle for political loyalty?

Not really. When Shining Path first came on the scene, the Peruvian government was not the reformist force it is now (despite the suspension of democratic processes for a time by the Fujimori regime). It systematically ignored the interests of the Indians of the interior, to which Guzman's philosophy had some appeal. Although terrorism was part of Shining Path's tactics against intransigents (as almost always happens in insurgencies to some degree), it was not until it abandoned its ideology that it became as heavily dependent on terror as it is now. The Peruvian government, newly sensitive to the problem that spawned Shining Path in the first place, has made some progress in isolating and reducing the movement precisely because it has recognized the political aspect of counterinsurgency, something its predecessors ignored.

Counterinsurgency is also militarily difficult, because the government remains under siege as long as the insurgency exists as a military force. Whereas insurgents may eventually succeed by avoiding defeat and simply outlasting the will of the government to resist, counterinsurgents can only win by the total military defeat of the insurgents and the crushing of the insurgent's will to continue.

Overcoming enemy hostile ability is primarily a military task for which military force properly employed is the appropriate response. (An example of improper employment would be committing military acts that further alienate the population.) Hostile will—the animosity that underpins the political support for the insurgency—takes two forms. One form of hostile will that can be attacked is what I call *cost tolerance,* the unwillingness of one side to continue to endure the suffering inflicted by the other side. When one side decides that it would rather acquiesce to the demands of its opponent than to endure the consequences of resistance, then that party's cost tolerance has been exceeded. Overcoming hostile will defined as cost tolerance is the classic tactic of terrorists, who threaten continued mayhem (blowing up subway stations, for instance) until the target population gives in to their demands.

The assault on cost tolerance is both military and political. Militarily, it consists of taking action that causes the government and its supporters to suffer, preferably beyond their endurance. Politically, it consists of convincing the opponent that its interests are better served by quitting the contest.

The second sense of hostile will is the *embrace of the opponent's policies.* War, like any other political enterprise, involves policy preferences. In the case of insurgency-counterinsurgency, the basic political contest is over who shall rule and what policies the rulers will enact. One way to resolve basic differences may be to change who rules or to change policies so that both sides can embrace them, in which case there is no reason for continuing hostilities.

Understanding hostile ability and will helps frame the problem facing the counterinsurgent by specifying more clearly the political and military dimensions of the counterinsurgency problem. The counterinsurgents (normally the government) begin from the political standpoint of making and enforcing policies that some parts of the population find repulsive and unacceptable. One way to defuse the support base for the insurgency would be to moderate those policies, thereby facilitating their acceptance by those in opposition. In El Salvador, for instance, the basic grievance with the political system was the extreme maldistribution of land, with a handful of elite families controlling virtually all the arable land in a country where such land was in short supply. The intolerability of the situation formed the basis of the insurgency led by the Farabundo Marti National Liberation Front (FMLN).

One approach to the problem of land tenure in El Salvador was always land reform: changing the policies of the government to allow a more equitable distribution of land resources. But, as A. C. Bacevich and his colleagues pointed out in a particularly convincing fashion, that approach created a dilemma for the government, what he terms a tension between reform and repression. Policies obnoxious to one segment of the population must benefit some other segment (presumably the rulers and their supporters) to be instituted in the first place. The handful of large Salvadorean landholders also governed the country and created policies that protected their privilege. Engaging in political reform that would undercut support for the FMLN demanded their personal economic and political sacrifice, which they were unwilling to make.

The Dilemmas of Counterinsurgency

If one is unwilling to reform the system to meet the insurgency's demands (to attack the political base of its appeal), then one is left with military repression as the only way to end the insurgency. This creates the mindset that the insurgency is a military rather than a political problem, which distorts the dynamics of the situation and worsens the prospects of success.

The first problem that a strictly military approach creates is that counterinsurgency is conceptually as well as operationally more difficult than insurgency. Although technology has advanced and made possible counterinsurgent actions (such as rapid detection and engagement of small guerrilla units), most Second Tier governments have European-style military forces that are oriented toward the kind of large-unit, high-firepower warfare that mobile-guerrilla warfare is designed to defeat. Most governments also lack a reliable counterinsurgency doctrine.

The second problem is that decimating insurgent forces does not address the causes of insurgency: the political grievances that give rise to insurgency in the first place and, if unaddressed, provide its continuing rationale and appeal. As Bacevich puts it, "The short-range fix is to go up the hill and shoot the guerrilla; but that's addressing the effect, not the cause."

The third problem is that a purely military approach is probably too incomplete and unsophisticated to address the social and political problem in its entirety. The result may well be the failure to eradicate the insurgency and hence to become bogged down in a war of attrition, which is exactly what the insurgents want. It may also breed a sort of fatalistic bunker mentality and a cynicism of purpose. As D. Michael Shafer suggested several years ago: "For certain elites the aim of fighting is to defend power and privilege and thus the prescribed good government (democratic, responsive, law-abiding, corruption-free) may be even less palatable than toughing out the insurgency as long as possible before flying to exile in Miami or Monaco." Although the quote was published in 1988, it sounds eerily like the situation in Haiti in 1994, where General Raoul Cedras and his coup brethren held out and bled the body politic dry before submitting to exile.

Phases of Counterinsurgency

According to Bacevich et al., proper counterinsurgent activities generally proceed (including any outside interference that may occur) in two sequential but contradictory phases. The first phase consists of avoiding defeat at the hands of the insurgents. The general problem is that governments either ignore or improperly approach insurgency in its early stages—engaging, for instance, in the kinds of large-unit actions that guerrillas generally avoid—and allow the insurgency to progress through the second stage of mobile-guerrilla warfare. This tendency is particularly true for outside states perceiving an interest in the counterinsurgency. The dynamic is what Todd Greentree calls the "counterinsurgency contradiction": the tendency of governments to ignore situations or view them as inconsequential until they become critical, at which point involvement is unlikely to succeed.

The insurgency has usually entered the third and critical phase by the time a concerted counterinsurgency is mounted. At this point, the insurgents have reorganized as large military units (or called out the conventional forces they have been reserving for the propitious moment) in order to administer the military coup de main and topple the government. If the insurgents have correctly concluded that the government's forces are so depleted that they will not be able to resist the onslaught (like the South Vietnamese armed forces in 1975, for instance), then only outside intervention may save the day for the counterinsurgents. (This was the apparent effect of introducing American troops in large numbers into Vietnam in 1965, when the North Vietnamese and their Viet Cong allies first entered the third phase.) The counterinsurgents must engage in heavy, large-unit counterattacks, the purpose of which is "killing bold and aggressive guerrillas . . . to deprive them, at least momentarily, of the ability to seize power," in Bacevich's words. The counterinsurgency's goal here is simply to avoid extinction. If it fails, the insurgency prevails. If it succeeds, ironically enough, it may teach the wrong lessons for the continued conduct of the counterinsurgency.

If the counterinsurgents succeed in deflecting the final offensive, then in all likelihood (assuming they follow their own doctrine), the insurgents will retreat strategically into phase two of mobile-guerrilla strategy, the guerrilla phase. The problem is that success in stopping the final offensive is likely to reinforce a reliance on the large-unit tactics that were successful in opposing the conventionally configured insurgents. This success triggers a phenomenon that Greentree refers to as the "brushfire corollary": the assumption that, like brushfires, guerrilla wars can be controlled, even extinguished, by the maximum application of military force. Moreover, large-unit engagements are directed by senior-level officers, who get the credit for success and may therefore become enamored with such tactics. Success may then reinforce the predeliction to continue military repression as the means of overcoming the insurgency.

The requirements for the second phase of counterinsurgency are quite different than those for the first phase. With the insurgency returned to its guerrilla phase, the competition between the government and the insurgents returns to the politico-military battle for the allegiance of the citizenry. Large-unit campaigns (such the armored search-and-destroy missions conducted by the United States in Vietnam that met with so little success) need to give way to small-unit activities whereby relatively small, highly mobile government units pursue and capture or destroy equally small guerrilla bands—essentially countering guerrillas by imitating what they do. This is often unpopular with the military leadership, because operational command reverts to a much lower point in the officer corps (captains and below), and there are relatively few large operations for the upper echelon to command.

For the counterinsurgency to make more than the most transitory progress during this phase, it must generously intermix political and military actions, with an emphasis on the former. According to the U.S. Army's FM 100-20, this calls for four things: unity of effort ("coordinated effort and centralized control at all levels," principally to avoid taking actions that will further alienate the population); the maximum use of intelligence information "as the basis of all action"; *minimum use of violence* (italics added); and responsive government.

The best form of counterinsurgency is good government. Insurgencies stand little chance of getting started and even less of prospering in societies marked by well respected, honest governments that are trying responsibly to govern their countries in ways that will benefit all or most of their citizens. When these conditions are met, there will be no need for a counterinsurgency strategy. Where all or most of those conditions are unmet, it is hard to imagine counterinsurgency succeeding unless one side or another changes. As Shafer puts it, the "three oughts" of successful counterinsurgency are security of the people from insurgent coercion, "competent, legal responsive administration free from past abuse" (good government), and progress in meeting "rising population expectations with higher living standards."

Counterinsurgency and New Internal War

There may be a partial exception to the previous discussion that may also provide clues as to how the system will operate in the future. That exception is El Salvador. In that eleven-year war, neither side won and neither lost decisively. The government was supported and armed by the United States, with numerous American advisers on the scene directing and offering assistance. To complete the Cold War overlay, the Soviets supported the insurgents, funneling arms through Cuba and Nicaragua until the fall of the Sandanistas and the demise of the Soviet Union. For most of the war, the Salvadoran elite resisted any reforms that would deprive them of their power and privilege, preferring a military solution that remained elusive. In the end, the two sides laid down their arms and reached a compromise solution. Insurgencies are not supposed to end that way.

The central factors include the loss of Cold War support and exhaustion from a long and arduous experience. The FMLN lost its source of support most obviously when Gorbachev began scaling back assistance, and conclusively when the Soviet Union ceased to exist. The rebels thus had every incentive to negotiate before the lack of supplies led to their defeat. At the same time, the absence of Soviet interference reduced the need for the United States to put up with the Salvadorans' refusal to reform the corrupt land-tenure system (something the United States had been urging for years). The Americans could thus tell the government in San Salvador to go to the table or be on their own. Since both sides had been fighting for so long, sheer exhaustion must have played a role as well: Almost everyone wanted the war ended.

What, then, does "classic" counterinsurgency tell us about dealing with the new internal wars? The Salvadoran example may be instructive for dealing with insurgencies that date back to the Cold War. Tentative (if reversible) progress toward ending conflicts in such places as Angola (currently being brokered by the United States) and Mozambique may display the dual impact of the loss of patron support and sheer exhaustion from the effort.

The application of classic insurgency-counterinsurgency reasoning is much more tenuous in kinds of conflicts I have described as new internal wars. The lynchpin that ties together insurgency and counterinsurgency is the moderating impact of a common center of gravity that must be simultaneously attacked and protected for fear of alienating the common populace. That dynamic, as well as the quest to politically convert the adversary population, is sadly missing in such places as Rwanda and Bosnia, where conversion is not even an afterthought. For those places, the model is Cambodia, not Vietnam.

If there is limited applicability of classic insurgency and counterinsurgency practice and theory in the new internal war, then the vital question is whether the lessons of outside involvement—and especially physical intervention—in insurgent warfare during the Cold War offers usable guidance for the new internal wars.

PROSPECTS FOR EXTERNAL INTERVENTION IN NEW INTERNAL WAR

To assess the current practicality of external intervention it is helpful to compare the "war" in Somalia with the war in Vietnam. In both cases, missions led by the United States failed miserably to attain the political objectives they set out to accomplish. In Vietnam, the original objective was to ensure a noncommunist South Vietnam; after Richard Nixon's Vietnamization policy became the defining purpose, the objective was limited to a *reasonable prospect* of South Vietnamese independence. In either case, the United States failed utterly.

It is not clear what the political objective was in Somalia. Certainly part of it was to alleviate the great suffering of the Somali people, but that was a tactical objective; the real problem in Somalia, of which the human-induced campaign of starvation was the weapon of choice, was political anarchy. Ending the starving by reopening the transportation system that could get food to those in need was a stopgap measure to allow stabilization and then to engage in state building that might leave a more prosperous, and certainly more stable, Somali polity in which the tragedy would not be repeated. Ironically, attaining the first objective was possible but ultimately not decisive; attaining the second was important and necessary but unattainable. U.S. intervention treated the symptom for a time; it utterly failed (to the extent it consciously tried) to build a new Somali state. In retrospect officials estimate the number of Somalis who did not starve because of the American-led effort at around 100,000; they are silent on the extent to which Somalia is a better place after a long and expensive international involvement.

The legacies of the two experiences are also parallel. The lesson of Vietnam was "no more Vietnams," and the meaning of that lesson has been discussed for over twenty years. For a decade (until Ronald Reagan voided it in Lebanon and Grenada in 1983) it meant no more involvements in Third World civil wars. Since then, politicians, theoreticians, and military analysts have been attempting to refine the list of circumstances in which involvement might not necessarily be doomed to failure. The result is the body of insurgency theory discussed in this chapter.

The parallel lesson of Somalia is "no more Somalias"; in the immediate wake of American participation in the UN mission in Somalia (UNISOM) this has meant no more involvement in active shooting wars in the Second Tier (assuming that American participation in supervising the Bosnian peace can be described in standard peacekeeping terms). What has yet to occur is the second phase of response where we attempt to gain a more discriminating and sophisticated view of when it is possible (if at all) to think about positive intervention in new internal wars.

The Dynamics of Outside Intervention

During the Cold War, the experience of outsiders intervening to thwart insurgencies was not encouraging. In fact, since 1945, there has not been a single instance of a successful intervention by a racially distinct intervenor in a civil war employing the mobile-guerrilla strategy where the insurgents enjoyed a level of indigenous support and where the insurgency had successfully entered the second stage of guerrilla fighting.

This categorical statement does not mean all insurgencies succeed or that all interventions fail. What it does say is that outside intervention is unlikely to succeed in situations where an unpopular government is besieged by a rebellion that enjoys reasonable popular support. In these circumstances, outsiders are unlikely to be the critical element in turning around the situation. As Sir Robert Thompson, the architect of the successful counterinsurgency in Malaya (which is not an exception to the assertion in the previous paragraph, because the insurgents were mostly ethnic Chinese who did not have the support of the Malay people), put it in his memoir: "There is no hope of democracy and stability if nothing works. Reliance on a military solution will always fail, *particularly when sought by foreign troops*" (emphasis added).

There are several justifications for this assessment. The first arises from Greentree's democratic contradiction. Unless the situation in a target country is truly desperate, it may be difficult to build a sufficient "domestic consensus" (to borrow from Sam Sarkesian) in the potential intervenor's country to mount an effort. When the task might be manageable, there is unlikely to be much support, particularly if American or other vital interests are not apparent. Thus, there is a tendency to wait until the situation is beyond mediation before action is seriously contemplated. The contradiction also dictates that the government appear worthy of redemption, a condition also difficult to attain unless concern with its beleaguerment is well accepted.

A second problem has to do with the limited influence an outside party can have. One aspect of this is the extent to which the United States, or any country, can influence the conduct of governance in the target country. If the institution of political reforms is perceived as required to undercut the insurgency and the government chooses to resist reform (which was the problem the United States encountered in Vietnam when Ngo Dinh Diem was president), there is little prospect that the intervention will succeed. As Shafer puts it, "Americans cannot control the political, administrative and military machinery of allied governments." Moreover, the brushfire corollary analogy can lead to the assessment that a large dousing of superior military force will solve the problem, which is a dubious proposition at best.

The third problem is the inverse relationship between the level of outside involvement and the amount of leverage the intervenor has over the government it is seeking to protect. The relationship between levels of involvement and success has to do principally with the apparent desperation of the government being assisted. If the government cannot conduct the counterinsurgency on its own and must rely progressively on outsiders to carry out its fight, it probably commands a low level of support and legitimacy. As FM 100-20 argues, "The burden of carrying the conflict must remain with the government or the insurgents. To do otherwise is to 'Americanize' the conflict, destroying the legitimacy of the entity we are attempting to assist. . . . Responsibility for the counterinsurgency must remain with the host government if its legitimacy is to survive." In other words, the more intervention is needed, the less likely it is to be effective, because the more evident the intervention is, the greater the weakness of the government must be.

This inverse relationship also extends to the amount of leverage that the intervenor has over the host government, a problem that was particularly evident in Vietnam. When a country intervenes in an internal war, it automatically gains a stake in the outcome: If the intervention was justified in the first place (which it must be in political democracies), then so too must be the outcome. The problem is that the stakes increase as the investment increases, and the host government is likely (and correctly) to conclude that it can ignore admonitions in areas such as reform. The only threat the intervenor can make in the absence of compliance is its withdrawal, which it cannot do without at least tacitly admitting to its own public that the intervention was wrong in the first place.

This point should serve as a warning to any country contemplating intervention in another country's internal war. If the existence of an insurgency is itself testimony to a malaise within the government that must ultimately be resolved politically, and if the government is likely to resist changes that will take away its privileges, then the intervenor's inability to exert leverage over that government can only lead to frustration. Moreover, if this problem is manifested in military setbacks that only the intervenor can attempt to reverse, the situation can only be described as one of progressive deterioration.

The final difficulty of outside intervention is the likelihood that the intervenor and the host government will have contradictory purposes in conducting the counterinsurgency. This will often arise from a disagreement over policy: reform versus repression, for example. If the government resists reform for fear of losing its privileges, then it will view the problem in military terms and will desire the intervenors to eradicate the insurgents physically. The intervenor, on the other hand, is likely to see the solution as state building, which requires the reforms the government resists. Unless the government and the intervenor can reach accord on the nature of the problem and the means of its solution, the result is likely to be continuing frustration in their relations and in attaining a successful conclusion.

CONCLUSIONS: INTERVENTION IN NEW INTERNAL WAR

If the pattern of new internal wars differs from that of classic insurgency, the dynamics of intervention may not. There is not enough history of intervention in this new phenomenon to discern a pattern or to make categorical assertions, but even this limited experience suggests that it may be just as difficult to intervene successfully in the new internal wars as in more standard insurgencies.

The analogy between Vietnam and Somalia again offers some suggestions. To analyze the problem of intervention in Vietnam-style wars, I devised (in *Distant Thunder*) a set of six questions a potential intervener might ask itself before becoming involved. Applying those questions to Somalia (which might not have been a bad idea before the commitment was made) may start to suggest the parallels.

1. *What is wrong here?* In Somalia, the apparent problem was massive impending starvation, which the American-led UN relief operation proposed to alleviate. The deeper problem was a condition of anarchy that the contending parties had been unable to resolve (and still have not). Reinstating the flow of grain was a temporary solution, which certainly saved many lives but did not, and could not, solve the chronic Somali inability to govern itself in peace.

2. *How do you come down on the "side of the angels?"* How does one determine the side worthy of support? In the context of the Cold War, one could assign fealty based upon the profession of communism or anticommunism. That distinction is missing in the post–Cold War world, and potential conflicts may occur in places about which one has little knowledge (and less interest); determining who deserves support may therefore be exceedingly difficult. It is, for instance, impossible to determine who the United States viewed as worthy of American support in Somalia when the SEALS and Marines churned ashore.

3. *Does your side have a reasonable chance of winning?* This question, of course, presupposes that one has identified a side to support. One of the variations that post–Cold War involvement tends to take, however, is that of UN-style peacekeeping. The classic peacekeeping mission is ostensibly neutral and evenhanded, but it is not clear that neutrality can be maintained in the absence of a sincere desire for peace. In such circumstances, the operative role is termed peace enforcement, a euphemism that implies there is a peace to enforce, though normally the condition is war. Such a situation inevitably places the intervenor on one side or the other regardless of its origi-

nal intent. The United States did not enter Somalia with the intent of opposing Mohammed Farah Aidid; when the mission led to disarming militias in Mogadishu, however, that is exactly what happened.

4. *Do you recognize the limits on your ability to influence the outcome?* This question arises directly from the discussion in the previous section regarding the amount of leverage and the effect the intervenor can have. In many of the new internal wars, the central problem is the absence of effective governance by whatever government is in power, combined with the absence of any form of coherent governing alternative among the insurgents. In these conditions of failed statehood, the principal problem thus becomes state building, a task for which military forces have no particular expertise. This is the ongoing problem in Somalia.

5. *Do you have a viable politico-military strategy?* This question gets to the heart of the purpose of this chapter. Over time and with experience, a strategy has been developed for approaching and dealing with conventional insurgency. If, as has been suggested, the dynamics of new internal wars are different from those of conventional insurgencies, then new strategies may have to be designed.

6. *What will the American people say about involvement?* In a democratic system this is the ultimate question and, as argued in Chapter 1, the principal limitation on the application of military force by First Tier countries. Although it is less than crystal clear what the public will and will not support, the evident revulsion with the Somalian adventure, the apparent disinterest in the Rwandan massacre, and the great reluctance to become involved in the Bosnian tragedy suggest that there is less than consensual support for such actions.

This chapter has summarized how the West, and particularly the United States, came to view involvement in conventional insurgencies during the Cold War, and has suggested that new internal war may present a somewhat different problem requiring somewhat different solutions. Chapter 4 specifies the emerging characteristics of new internal wars, and especially how they differ from conventional insurgencies. The discussion will then turn to how the international system, and especially the countries of the First Tier, may come to view this phenomenon.

REFERENCES

Bacevich, A. J. et al. *American Military Policy in Small Wars: The Case of El Salvador.* Cambridge, Mass.: Institute for Foreign Policy Analysis, 1989.

Giap, Vo Nguyen. *People's War, People's Army.* New York: Praeger, 1962.
Gorbachev, Mikhail S. *Perestroika: New Thinking for Our Country and the World.* New York: Harper and Row, 1987.
Greentree, Todd. *The United States and the Politics of Conflict in the Developing World.* Washington, D.C.: U.S. Department of State Center for the Study of Foreign Affairs, 1990.
Guevara, Ernesto ("Che"). *Guerrilla Warfare.* New York: Monthly Review Press, 1961.
Mao tse-Tung, *Collected Works.* Peking: People's Publishing House, 1965.
Paschall, Rod. *LIC 2010: Special Operations and Unconventional Warfare in the Next Century.* Washington, D.C.: Brassey's, 1990.
Sarkesian, Sam. *America's Forgotten Wars: The Counterrevolutionary Past and Lessons for the Future.* Westport, Conn.: Greenwood Press, 1984.
Shafer, D. Michael. *Deadly Paradigms: The Failure of U.S. Counterinsurgent Policy.* Princeton, N.J.: Princeton University Press, 1988.
———. "The Unlearned Lessons of Counterinsurgency." *Political Science Quarterly* 103, 1 (Spring 1988): 57–80.
Snow, Donald M. *Distant Thunder: Third World Conflict and the New International Order.* New York: St. Martin's Press, 1993.
Snow, Donald M. and Dennis M. Drew. *From Lexington to Desert Storm: War and Politics in the American Experience.* Armonk, N.Y.: M. E. Sharpe, 1994.
Sun Tzu. *The Art of War.* Translated by Samuel B. Griffith. Oxford, U.K.: Oxford University Press, 1963.
Thompson, Sir Robert. *Make for the Hills: Memoirs of Far Eastern Wars.* London: Lee Cooper, 1989.
U.S. Army, *Guide to the Study of Insurgency.* Ft. Huachuca, Ariz., 1989.

4

New Internal Wars

We are not yet far removed from the Cold War and the effects it had on the Second Tier, including the pattern of violence it sometimes spawned and other times regulated and moderated. 1992 was the first year the Cold War overlay disappeared completely as an international political influence on the violence I have identified as new internal war. New internal war is an evolving phenomenon, the exact dimensions of which are not entirely clear. Some of the violence in the current system appears different from that of the past; this contrast is evident in the political characteristics of these conflicts and in their military conduct. But because it is such a recent phenomenon, one can describe these wars only in an inductive manner.

These wars can be assigned to two periods. First are those wars (or problems) that originated before the end of the Cold War but have continued into the post–Cold War world. Three distinctly different examples stand out. One is the ongoing struggle of the Kurds, principally in Iraq and Turkey. The cause of Kurdish nationalism, and the struggle to realize or suppress Kurdish statehood dates back in modern times at least to the presentation of demands for a Kurdish state at the Versailles conference settling World War I. Those demands have consistently lacked a powerful sponsor to aid in their realization. The American-led Operation Provide Comfort has created de facto independence for Iraqi Kurds, but that independence will last only as long as the American, British, and French air forces are available to prevent the imposition of Iraqi sovereignty over what is universally admitted to be the sovereign territory of Iraq that comprises Iraqi Kurdistan. Fighting rages periodically in eastern Turkey where Turkish Kurds attempt at least autonomy; their cause is unaided, officially because the Kurdish movement in Turkey espouses a Marxist ideology but also because Turkey is a NATO ally that the First Tier feels should not be alienated. With deep roots in irredentism, however, the various aspects of the Kurdish struggle can be thought of as classic insurgency in the Cold War mode.

The other examples of this period conform more closely to the perception of a new form of internal war. In Liberia, what began as a purported civil war in 1990 (led by Charles Taylor) quickly degenerated into little more than a criminal insurgency whose principal activities involved terrorizing the countryside. The net result has been to destroy the once prosperous (at least by African standards) Liberian economy and to send much of the economically productive population into exile from which they may or may not return now that a peace of sorts has been reached. Outside interference in this "war" was minimal, partially because Liberia had never been subject to a colonial power that might retain residual interest. The United States, as Liberia's occasional patron, limited its involvement to a special-forces raid to extract threatened embassy and other personnel from the conflict zone. The Liberian model serves as a prototype for similar actions in central Africa. Although a formal reconciliation between factions in 1995 created the semblance of a government and peace, the countryside remained a war zone.

A third ongoing example involves a hybrid of sorts in Sudan. The civil conflict there began in 1983, when a radically Islamic, militarily dominated government came into power on the promise of creating an Islamically pure society. The government seeks both to crush the rebellion between itself and the two wings of the Sudanese People's Liberation Army (which split in 1991, one group advocating regional autonomy and the other outright secession) and to religiously purify Sudan. The rebels are either Christians or animists and are principally residents of the southern part of Sudan, although the conflict has tragically spread to the Nuba mountains as well.

On the surface, the war may seem unremarkable, little different from the Ethiopian attempt to prevent Eritrean secession (although in the Ethiopian case, a Christian government sought to suppress—some would argue extinguish—a rebellious Muslim population). Two characteristics place the Sudanese case into the category of new internal war. The first is the savage, genocidal quality that the war has taken. The ruling Islamic government has declared the struggle a holy war (jihad) and has even issued an edict (*fatwa*) justifying the murder of civilians on religious grounds. According to Julie Flint, reporting in London's *The Independent* (reproduced in *World Press Review*), the *fatwa* says: "An insurgent who was once a Muslim is now an apostate [someone who has forsaken his or her religion]. A non-Muslim is a non-believer standing as a bulwark against the spread of Islam. And Islam has granted the freedom of killing both." The second characteristic is that the Sudanese government has successfully managed to suppress outside media coverage of the carnage to an extent that should be the envy of tyrants everywhere. There is little sense of external rage at the Sudanese government largely because the world is unaware of the events transpiring in that country.

The second period includes those conflicts that were either spawned by the breakup of the Cold War or have begun since the Cold War ended. The most prominent examples of the former are the violent conflicts that have occurred either in the successor states of the Soviet Union or in the Balkans. Both cases share a resurgence of exclusionary nationalism that had been suppressed (or, many people erroneously thought, extinguished) by the long period of communist rule. Within the successor states, examples include the Abkhazian attempt at secession from Georgia (a problem by no means completely resolved), the attempt by Armenia to unite a Christian Armenian enclave within Muslim Azerbaijan with Armenia (Nagorno Karabakh), and the similar attempt by Azerbaijan to reattach a Muslim enclave separated from Azerbaijan by a portion of Armenia (Nakichevan). This conflict could take on greater global significance with the movement to tap huge oil and natural-gas reserves (reportedly the second largest in the world) under the Caspian Sea but under Azerbaijani sovereign control. The Islamic fundamentalist movement in Tajikistan parallels the more highly publicized campaigns in Algeria and Egypt. Within the Balkans the long, bloody war of ethnic cleansing and land grabbing has dominated the scene.

Examples of wars that have begun or come into public view since the end of the Cold War include the situation in Sierre Leone. The conflict actually began in March 1991, when the Revolutionary United Front (RUF) began operations in opposition to the government of Joseph Momoh. The original stated purpose of the RUF uprising was the institution of multiparty democracy. When Momoh was overthrown by a military junta whose primary goal was to eradicate the RUF, the movement retreated to a campaign of lawlessness and destabilization.

These examples of new internal war demonstrate some differences from classic insurgent warfare. We now turn our attention to some political and military characteristics of these wars and the kinds of states in which they occur.

NEW INTERNAL WAR–PRONE SOCIETIES

Project Ploughshares keeps a record of "major armed conflicts," which it defines as ongoing armed fighting in which at least cumulative deaths have occurred. Through the end of 1993, conflicts meeting that definition were ongoing in thirty-eight countries; some of these date back quite far (India to 1947, Israel to 1948). Of the total, twenty-seven began before the fall of the Berlin Wall in November 1989; the remaining eleven began between that date and the end of 1993.

Table 4.1 places the Project Ploughshares data within the framework of tiers and distinguishes those states falling within and outside the general prosperity (at least promised) of the proposed economic associations that may be the defining boundaries of the global economy.

Table 4.1 Distribution of Internal Conflicts

First Tier States: 1
Free Trade Area of the Americas: 4
Asia-Pacific Economic Cooperation: 3
Other areas: 30
  Africa: 13
  Formerly communist countries: 6
  Southern Asia: 4
  Middle East: 7
Total: 38

Some explanation of this distribution may be helpful. The one instance of a First Tier state with an ongoing civil war is the United Kingdom's war over Northern Ireland. Among the Middle Eastern states, three of the reported conflicts (Israel, Iran, and Iraq) have both internal and international dimensions. The only other conflict in the survey that arguably is not internal is part of Croatia's involvement in the general war over Bosnia and Herzegovina (although Croatian Serbs who have been removed from the Krajina region would clearly contend there is a strong internal element to the war there).

The Global Economy and New Internal Wars

The notion of the economic prosperity and extension of the global economy through participation in one or another of the free-trading areas holds up well in this distribution. As the table shows, only four of the thirty-four members of the proposed Free Trade Area of the Americas (FTAA), Colombia, Guatemala, Haiti, and Peru, have ongoing internal wars, and these generally meet the criteria of being new, as opposed to classic, civil conflicts: The conflicts in Peru and Colombia are narco-insurgencies, and Haiti is a classic case of a failed state. The sporadic fighting in Guatemala is the only conflict being contested in more or less the Cold War pattern.

Largely the same is true of countries that make up the Asia-Pacific Economic Cooperation (APEC). There are eighteen members of that association, three of which are embroiled in internal war of one sort or another. Indonesia and Papua New Guinea have secessionist movements that belong to the newer phenomenon, whereas the war being waged by the New People's Army against the government of the Philippines is the only classic insurgency in that region.

The thirty remaining conflicts are being fought in those parts of the world that are outside the areas of growing economic prosperity. They are, as the table indicates, geographically concentrated in four areas: the bulk in Africa, with smaller but significant numbers in the Middle East, South Asia, and the successor states to the Soviet Union and the Balkans.

The pattern for those countries outside the global economy generally holds in terms of subtiers of the Second Tier. In Africa, for instance, ten of the thirteen wars are within countries listed as developable (Burundi, Chad, Kenya, Liberia, Mozambique, Rwanda, Sierre Leone, Somalia, Sudan, and Zaire). Of the remaining three in Africa, one occurs in a developed Second Tier country (South Africa), one in a partially developed state (Angola), and one in a resource-rich country (Algeria).

The same pattern holds for the formerly communist world and south Asia. Within the formerly communist world, four of the five are in the developable subtier: Azerbaijan (which will join the resource rich once exploitation of its reserves begins), Bosnia and Herzegovina, Georgia, and Tajikistan. Croatia, a partially developed state, is the exception. Within south Asia, six of the seven are developable (Afghanistan, Bangladesh, Burma/Myanmar, Cambodia, Laos, and Sri Lanka); partially developed India is the exception.

The only area that confounds the classification method is the Middle East. In that region, one of the five states involved in internal conflict is in the developed subtier (Israel), two are partially developed (Lebanon and Turkey), and two are resource rich (Iran and Iraq). This deviation can be explained partly by the ideosyncratic pattern of Middle Eastern conflict along religious lines (Muslims versus Jews, Sunni versus Shiite Muslims, fundamentalists within both Islamic traditions). At the same time, only two of the thirteen states in the Middle East (Jordan and Yemen) are classified as developable, and both have a history of internal conflict.

These statistics generally support the suggestion that internal wars are concentrated in the poorest parts of the world, and especially in those parts of the world most distant from the global economy. The majority of those countries experiencing internal wars are the poorest—in the developable subtier. This is clearest among those outside the First Tier/FTAA/APEC axis: twenty-one of thirty wars in those countries involve developable countries. Of the eight within the global economy, three (the Philippines, Haiti, and Peru) are occurring in developable countries, which brings the total to twenty-four out of thirty-eight.

One may argue that this is a condition for internal war generally, given that the majority of the reported conflicts began during the Cold War period. I would not take exception, but would assert that the pattern *does diverge from that suggested by the development literature of the Cold War period.* Had the revolution of rising expectations been a determining factor, one would expect a greater concentration of internal wars within the partially developed subtier, whereas only six out of the thirty-eight are occurring in partially developed countries (India, Lebanon, Turkey, Colombia, Croatia, and Angola). The economic factor is important to understanding the totality of the problem and to devising strategies for alleviating the conditions that lead to these kinds of wars.

Internal war, old or new, tends to occur in the most economically wretched of places, where the so-called misery index is likely to be at its highest and the stakes to be lowest. This is particularly true of the criminal insurgencies of central Africa, where marauding bands are competing for extraordinarily small caches of wealth. Such "wars" also drive away what little prosperity there may be, as was the case in Liberia and Sierre Leone; it is extraordinarily unlikely that development through private investment will occur. In the case of narco-insurgencies there are large amounts of money to be made for the drug dealers, but relatively little of it finds its way down to the "insurgents" who protect them and even less to the coca growers.

Political Environment

On the political side of the internal war environment two phenomena stand out: the frequency of these wars in the so-called failed states of the system, and some ethnic/nationalist justification for the wars. The term "failed state" has only recently entered the lexicon of international relations and its acceptance is not universal. The definition of a failed state put forward by Gerald Helman and Steven Ratner is a state "utterly incapable of sustaining itself as a member of the international community." Failed states, in other words, are those states that for economic, political, or, more usually, both reasons show little chance of becoming productive, prosperous, and stable members of the system. In their worst instances, they are states in which economic misery for the vast majority is coupled with virtual governmental anarchy.

If the name failed state is new, the phenomenon is not. During the Cold War, to the concepts of First, Second, and Third Worlds was occasionally added the category of Fourth World to describe those states with no meaningful prospects of completing the development process. There is a clear differentiation between states in the developable subtier of the Second Tier. There is a series of states whose per capita incomes hover near the $1,000 mark and whose economies show signs of diversifying and moving toward the first industrial revolution. There is also a collection of states within the subtier whose per capita income stagnates at $200 to $400, whose economic activity is largely limited to subsistence agriculture, and whose little foreign exchange is earned by selling food, from mineral extraction, or, in a few cases, by tourism. The appendix of Snow and Brown, *The Contours of Power,* reveals the number of such cases to be depressingly large. There is little likelihood that these states will progress upward through the subtiers without massive public or private investment, which their circumstances are almost guaranteed not to attract.

When states fail, the results can be devastating to the inhabitants, and the problem can and often does spill beyond state borders, involving the greater international community in an attempt to end the violence that often attends failure. It is therefore necessary to define the meaning and dynamics of failure and to specify the places where it has or may occur.

Not all very poor states fall into the category of failed states. Rather, one should think of the failed states as a subset of the old Fourth World that consists of those countries that are *both* economically and politically destitute. Economic misery serves as a necessary condition for the political failure of the state: People generally do not, for instance, rebel against improved or improving conditions. At the same time, economic misery is not itself a sufficient condition for the state to fail.

Failed states may be classified into three categories: failed states, failing states, and states with the potential to fail.

Failed States

The *failed states* are those in which governance has broken down and virtual anarchy (often taking the form of extremely brutal rule by elements utterly lacking in legitimacy) has persisted across time. Such circumstances may be manifested in chaotic internal violence in an attempt to gain political control or even to destroy political authority. The prototypical failed state, for which the term was devised (in much the same way that Charles Krauthammer created the term "weapon state" to describe Iraq), is Somalia. That country, like much of the rest of the Horn of Africa, is desperately poor, and the drought of the latter 1980s made the situation even more desperate. It is also a country that is perpetually unstable; the rule of thumb is that when one clan or coalition of clans is strong enough to impose authoritarian rule, then there is something resembling order (if not legitimacy). When, as was the case after Siad Barre was overthrown in 1991, no clan or clans can capture power, the result is virtual political chaos. The "war" in Somalia has been conventional in the sense that the seizure of political power is the objective of at least the major contending clans; it is unconventional in that there is little apparent attempt at political conversion beyond random terrorism.

Somalia is the prototype, but by no means the only instance of a failed state. Although an agreement between contending groups in Liberia in September 1995 appeared to end the chaotically violent, largely criminal insurgency that left the country essentially ungoverned for some years, the peace is uneasy. One Liberian leader, Charles Taylor, reportedly spoke of the war to American UN Ambassador Madeleine Albright during a visit to Monrovia in January 1996: "I started it, and now I don't know how to stop it" (quoted by Thomas L. Friedman in a January 26, 1996, *New York Times* column). Despite international efforts to bring about a settlement, Bosnia remained a failed state from the breakup of Yugoslavia until the U.S.-brokered peace process produced a shaky accord. The situation could easily return to a land grab when international forces are withdrawn. Prior to the imposition of an American force in Haiti that allowed reinstatement of President Aristide, Haiti had a long history of essential anarchy or rule by thuggery. Rwanda, and Cambodia under the Khmer Rouge, easily falls into the same category.

These examples share several characteristics. First, the conflicts occurred in poor states that lacked any sense of common political loyalty or affiliation. That does not mean that nationality or ethnicity—the popular shibboleths of recent literature—were always prominent. There is no ethnic divide among Somalis, Cambodians, or Haitians, whose common trait is the inability to govern themselves successfully. Ethnicity, or at least the manipulation of its symbols, was shared by the Bosnian and Rwandan tragedies, but it is by no means universal.

The second shared characteristic is that almost all attracted outside involvement, but with varied success. The intervention of Vietnam to topple the Khmer Rouge, and the ensuing UN-sponsored elections, have produced an apparently favorable outcome in Cambodia; the American-led occupation of Haiti has stabilized that country for the time being; and intervention in Somalia halted the starvation though it could do little to solve the underlying political chaos of the country. The system dithered for over three years in Bosnia before brokering a peace that will rely on the goodwill of all groups, an outcome easily predicted. Only in Liberia did the principals largely reach their own tentative accord.

The third shared characteristic of these situations is their fragility. Even in those cases in which apparent progress has been made there exists the likelihood of reversion. Haiti, for instance, has been unstable for a long time; can a six-months' occupation and crash course in democratization reverse nearly 200 years of Haitian political history? How fast will the memories fade among Bosnians regarding intergroup atrocity and brutality? Can Prince Sihanouk ride the wave to peace and prosperity? Will Liberia continue to swing between war and some level of order?

Failing and Potentially Failing States

The second category of failed state is that of the *failing states*, those countries that have yet to fall into a state of anarchy but are actively becoming failed states. Three states stand out as obvious candidates. Ethiopia lost its war to maintain control of Eritrea in 1993 following the overthrow of the authoritarian Dirgue regime in 1991. The country is desperately poor and has not been able to achieve a consensus on a successor regime. Georgia, despite the heroic efforts of its president, Eduarde Shevardnadze, and the occasional interference of the Russians, remains locked in what has become a debilitating, and apparently perpetual, war of attrition with Abkhazian separatists that threatens to throw the country into chaos. In Zaire, the rule of Mobutu Sese Seku has gradually deteriorated to the point that there is widespread anticipation in Africa of his imminent removal from office, which will result in a chaotic, tribally based civil war. A number of other central African states (Kenya, for instance) appear to be prime candidates for destabilization.

The third category is that of *states with the potential to fail*. This category includes those countries in which the ingredients for failure—economic misery, authoritarian rule—are in place but destabilization has not yet occurred. This dynamic is clearly present in a number of the successor states to the Soviet Union (especially the southern tier of successor states that face or border on Islamic central Asia) and in a number of other states that face challenges from Islamic fundamentalists. This latter challenge is especially frustrating, because the fervor, even fanaticism, of those seeking to purify Islamic states creates for them the justification to engage in what most consider particularly heinous acts of terrorism directed at civilian populations (and not restricted to the country in question, as the French have learned about Algerian extremists). The actions of such groups are paramilitary at best, and if they are shielded by sympathetic governments, they are difficult to penetrate and dismantle. The further fact that they do not directly seek to overthrow and replace governments makes them more difficult to deal with inside the framework of insurgency and counterinsurgency.

A major part of the political dynamic that appears to operate in these situations was introduced in Chapter 2. The basic notion is that destabilization, even devolution to the status of failed states, is most likely to occur when states with previously strong coercive capability (strong states) but weak societal consensus (weak societies) lose their coercive hold. The resulting deadly combination of weak states and societies can result in a political struggle that resembles the opening of the Oklahoma territory: a grab for as much power and support as possible in a state that is rapidly balkanizing into factions based on older and deeper forms of division.

Democratization and Ethnic Nationalism

This phenomenon has been complicated by the trend toward greater democratization, its intermingling with ethnic and nationalist sentiments, and assertions of the rights of self-determination expressed as the right to secession. It is difficult for Westerners to think of democratization—most prominently expressed as the freedom to discuss politics openly and without fear, and to participate in open elections—as having a negative side, but it can. Where there is little agreement among citizens on political matters—including who should rule and how—and this absence of consensus is reinforced by ethnic, national, tribal, and/or religious cleavages, then free expression can be negative, even brutal. When the veil of authoritarian rule is lifted, but no other agreed-upon forms of association are readily available to provide orderliness in people's lives, the tendency is to revert to older, more deeply held forms of association. In much of the former Soviet Union, for instance, there has been a reversion to pre-Soviet symbols, such as ethnicity and religion, both apparent anchors against a now rudderless existence.

The problem with the reemergence of nationalism in those parts of the world where weak societies exist is that it tends to be exclusionary rather than inclusive. *Inclusive nationalism* refers to national appeals (preferably coterminous with loyalty to the state) used to bring more and more groups into support for the general political system. Nationalism of this variety generally enhances the strength of the society by co-opting successive groups and thereby deepening and extending the legitimacy of the state.

With *exclusionary nationalism,* on the other hand, people of different nationalities associate themselves with subnational groups rather than with the state, and attempt to exclude members of other groups from their circle or, in more extreme cases, from political power or from the polity itself. This represents the darker side of national self-determination, when the cry to self-determine is used to justify ethnically pure states (true nation-states). At its worst, this is done by force, as in the "ethnic cleansing" campaigns undertaken in Bosnia to facilitate a postwar map in which Bosnians of different underlying ethnicities would predominate in different geographical areas. In the Bosnian case, the brutal military tactic of siege warfare, especially in Muslim-dominated cities like Sarajevo and Garadze, has been employed in the hope of forcing citizens to abandon their homes rather than continue to withstand the terrorist attacks by snipers and artillery.

Exclusionary nationalism also takes the form of attempts at secession. Examples of such attempts are found primarily in formerly communist countries such as the Soviet Union. These were not real states at all but empires conquered by force and then capriciously organized politically, so that multiple nationalities were placed within the so-called autuonomus republics, and ethnic groups were forcefully moved into areas in which they were unfamiliar and generally unwelcome. When the breakup of the empire occurred, some groups, such as the Ukrainians, quite naturally reasserted their claim to nationhood that predated the imperial reach of Soviet communism. Dividing the old Soviet Union into fifteen states was by no means enough for the exclusionary nationalists, who are attempting to carve out sovereign entities for themselves within Russia (the Chechens being merely the first to try) and within the other successor states.

This particular problem is not likely to go away. Although the Soviet breakup was advertised as the end of the imperial era, there are still large states that could face a similar fate to that of the Soviet Union. India, for instance, is an amalgam of any number of nationalities (Kashmiris, Sikhs, and Tamils to name three), many of whom are less than satisfied with their domination by the Indians. The possibility of China's dissolution, although it is overwhelmingly ethnically Chinese, in the absence of strong authoritarian rule by the communists is great (and this is, of course, how the communist party justifies its continued authoritarian rule). Almost all African states are multinational to some extent.

Particularly with the outbreak of an ostensibly ethnically based war in Bosnia, it became fashionable to describe internal wars in the Second Tier as if exclusionary nationalism was the overriding causative factor. It is true in some cases that wars within the failed states have ethnicity as their underlying cause, but ethnonationalist appeals are often as much instrumental as they are fundamental. In such places as Somalia ethnicity is not a factor at all.

It is the manipulation of long suppressed, in some cases probably forgotten, ethnonationalist differences for political purpose that marks the phenomenon at its most cynical and brutal. It is customary to take such a view of the war in Bosnia, which comes as close as any to an ethnic war, but the people of Bosnia whom we call Muslims, Serbs, or Croats have peacefully coexisted for many years together. Differences based in historical animosities (such as collaboration with or opposition to the Nazis in World War II, or Muslim cooperation with the Ottomans prior to World War I) have been dredged up to inflame politically motivated desires to acquire territory. Prior to the outbreak of war, however, it is difficult to imagine that the young men and women who have done the fighting and dying were strongly motivated by such concerns. The atrocities committed by all sides have created animosities and divisions that will be difficult to overcome, but they are as much the result as the cause of the war.

The other notable example of this phenomenon is the war in Rwanda, which many think of in almost purely ethnic terms. Certainly the killing involved Hutu rampages against the Tutsi (as well as Hutu sympathy with the Tutsi), and later Tutsi retaliation against the Hutu "militias" that had carried out the carnage, but was it based only on tribal hatred? The last time that Rwandans were designated Hutu or Tutsi was in the 1930s; that designation was not based on ethnic characteristics (over the 500 or so years that the Tutsi have lived in Rwanda, intermarriage has largely diluted ethnic purity) but rather on the number of cattle a person owned. Because of periodic fighting, however, conservative Hutu politicians were able to manipulate ethnic fears for the purpose of maintaining power.

The foregoing examples suggest that the underlying dynamics of new internal wars are somewhat different from those of conventional insurgencies during the Cold War. The focus now shifts to the ways those differences translate into a different pattern of politico-military action and justification.

POLITICAL AND MILITARY DIMENSIONS OF NEW INTERNAL WAR

A recent Council on Foreign Relations book (*Enforcing Restraint*, edited by Lori Fisler Damrosch) provides a much broader definition of internal war than has been used here. It classifies internal conflict as "ethnic strife, overthrow of an established government, disintegration of civil order, interference with humanitarian relief efforts, and other violence occurring within a state." This definition points to the array of violent activities taking place in states of the Second Tier and to the variety of problems and solutions they pose. However, the definition may be too broad.

The kinds of violent actions that have traditionally qualified as insurgencies fall within a single category of the list: overthrow of an armed government. The other categories represent the kinds of conflicts I have described as new internal wars. Ethnic conflict, civil disintegration, and interference with humanitarian relief efforts all make up the complex of actions that defies neat classification in traditional politico-military terms. They are the kinds of acts that one associates with the failed states and that give the new internal war its distinctively politically chaotic and militarily atrocious character. As one looked aghast at the genocide in Rwanda or the random atrocities against civilians in Sarajevo, one could not avoid observing that this was not warfare as we had known it. The new internal war simply does not conform to standard definitions of war. As a result, it is difficult to understand its political and military dimensions.

Political Characteristics of New Internal War

Although not all the internal wars that have dominated the post–Cold War landscape share all these characteristics, it is possible to discern at least five political distinctions between them and conventional insurgencies. Collectively, these characteristics describe a sense of political incoherence that undermines traditional notions of and the underlying purposes of war.

The first characteristic is a lack of clear political objectives framing the conflicts. In Cold War–era insurgencies, the objective was clear: to seize political power from a given government, generally according to some political rationale. In a number of contemporary internal wars, however, the articulation of a coherent political goal is implicit or derivative, if not missing altogether. They are similar to the apolitical wars of the pre-Westphalian period studied by historians such as John Keegan.

The internal conflicts in central Africa (Liberia, Sierre Leone, Kenya) are clearly of this nature. In Liberia, for instance, warfare broke out when Charles Taylor's National Patriotic Front of Liberia (NPFL) declared its intention to overthrow the rogue government of Samuel Doe in 1989. Although this was at least arguably a coherent political goal, an alternative political philosophy was never clearly articulated. The insurgency disintegrated into a largely criminal activity as the government and the rebels swept through and looted the country, sending most Liberians with sizable resources (needed to develop this very poor country) scurrying into exile. By the time some form of resolution was reached with a so-called unity government in late 1995, there was hardly anything left to govern. The Revolutionary United Front (RUF) of Sierre Leone has never articulated a political agenda of any kind, and manifestos of lofty political purpose have scarcely ennobled the causes in Kenya and Rwanda. If (or when) the government of Zaire finally destabilizes to the point of meltdown, there is likely to be a coherent drive for secession for Shaba province accompanied by political chaos throughout the rest of the country.

Without a clearly articulated political goal there is little if any political framework to limit the extent and nature of the violence that is committed. Violence in the name of Islamic virtue is political if its express purpose is to remove a government that violates the precepts of Muslim faith and proposes to replace the infidels with an alternative government that will reinstate the faith. If its purpose is stated in a *fatwa* that authorizes killing all nonbelievers (as in Sudan) or in random killing of women who fail to cover their heads properly (as in Algeria), then it is difficult to describe in conventional political terms. Similarly, the goal of creating ethnically pure communities in different parts of Bosnia is not so much a specific political goal as a justification for grabbing land.

The second characteristic is the absence of a discernible political ideology to justify the activity. One can argue that Cold War ideological justifications were little more than a cynical facade behind which those hungering for power sought to "sell" their appeal, but such ideology at least had a moderating effect as both sides attempted to appeal to portions of the population.

Political appeals are noticeably absent from a number of the new internal wars. The RUF of Sierre Leone does not bother to suggest to the citizenry that it should support them because they offer some superior governmental alternative, because that is not their purpose. Shining Path originally offered an ideology (if of a particularly lunatic variety) to entice political support; with the loss of its spiritual leader and its descent into criminality and terrorism, even the facade of popular appeal has disappeared. The only arguable exception is Islamic fundamentalism, which has the theocratic view that the state should promote Islamic purity.

The combined absence of clear political goals and ideology leads to the third and perhaps most important characteristic: the lack of a common center of gravity to which both the government and the insurgents must appeal. The new internal wars are not contests for the sympathy of a common population, but more closely resemble wars between states or even simple terrorism stripped of political motive. The ethnically based or justified violence of Rwanda is not encumbered by concern on the part of the Hutu that they may alienate the Tutsi; the Bosnian Serbs, Croats, or Muslims do not fear that forcing people from their residences would make political conversion or reconciliation more difficult. The violence is unmitigated by concern for the political consequences among the target population. Just as soldiers in interstate warfare are not terribly concerned that the enemy population will be negatively influenced, those seeking to commit genocide or to force population relocation are not concerned with the alienation of the victims. War becomes an independent, self-justifying activity.

A moderating appeal for popular support is also missing from the cases in Africa in which the existing order is destabilized to facilitate sheerly criminal activity, in the narco-insurgencies in Colombia and Peru to protect the narcotics trade from the government, or in Islamic fundamentalist violence against citizens who disagree with the views of the believers. The goal of these instances of new internal war is either to eradicate or to cow the target population. The result is the absence of constraint that makes these wars so terribly ferocious.

Consequences of Characteristics

The atrocities inspire international responses of horror and incredulity, and activate cries for humanitarian efforts to stop the slaughter.

One outcome has been to reactivate the war-crimes process for the first time since the aftermath of World War II. The tribunals currently at work over Bosnia and Rwanda are unlikely to be the last that are authorized, if more wars lacking common centers of gravity break out.

If the lack of political constraint characterizes many of these wars, they are further complicated by a demographic reality with enormous political consequences: the communal nature of habitation and settlement among contesting groups within war-torn societies. This problem has an antecedent in the Cold War period, in the Lebanese situation. The long and bloody war in Lebanon would have been easier to solve had it been possible to partition the Muslim and Christian communities. This would be similar to the Cypriot solution, which, if it has not exactly brought about a stable peace, has at least kept Greek and Turkish Cypriots away from each other's throats. The checkerboard pattern of habitation in Lebanon made such a solution impossible and contributed to the length and ferocity of the civil war. Ominously, only Syrian occupation could still the guns.

The same dynamic is at work in Bosnia and in other parts of the Balkans and the Soviet successor states. In the case of former Yugoslavia and the Soviet Union, intermingling was the result of conscious policy by the Tito and Stalin regimes, and its result is an integration of the population. When this is inflamed by nationalism there is a desire for exclusion that apparently can only be sated by forceful separation (ethnic cleansing) or by prolonged fighting until all sides become so exhausted that they prefer an imperfect peace to the continuation of war. This is national self-determination at its most hideous extreme.

Such conditions create an extremely intractable and frustrating experience for the parties involved and for the international community. Once passions are inflamed, the fighting tends to become especially furtive, particularly as atrocities between former neighbors accumulate and make the prospects for reconciliation more remote. How long will it be before the various factions in Bosnia will be able to trust and reconcile with one another? At the same time, even "successful" disengagement and relocation (never a pleasant experience, as Bell-Fialkoff among others has pointed out) leave imperfect borders that are difficult to secure. The inability to draw defensible borders in Bosnia contributed considerably to the difficulty of reaching an accord and, more fundamentally, of devising a peacekeeping scheme that could keep the parties apart.

The political reality of these situations is further complicated by the fact that the states in which the new internal wars occur are generally failed or failing. This means that the solution to the war involves not only stopping the fighting, which is only the symptom of the overriding problem of virtual or actual anarchy, but the more arduous task of building a viable state apparatus on which the citizens can agree. In the cases of the criminal or narcotics-based insurgencies, the basic underlying purpose is political impotency, either to create the lawlessness in which criminal acts can thrive or to facilitate the drug traffic. In such places as Haiti or Somalia, the lack of a tradition of good government impedes anything but temporary solutions. In states in transition from communist rule there are no accepted guidelines to assist in the nonviolent process of building viable and legitimate states.

Military Characteristics of New Internal War

The most striking military observation that one can make about a number of the new internal wars is how nonmilitary some of them seem. A few, such as the attempted Chechen and Abkhazian secessions, meet the standards of insurgency, although the Russian attempts at crushing the rebellion in Chechnya can hardly be classified as an attempt to win the hearts and minds of the Chechen population. Similarly, the war in Bosnia has many of the trappings of a conventional interstate war, even though it is ostensibly an internal war over the boundaries of Bosnia, Serbia/Yugoslavia, and Croatia.

Many of the new internal wars hardly resemble wars at all in any traditional sense. This is especially true of the criminal and narco-insurgencies in Africa and South America, the Islamic fundamentalist uprisings (which scarcely qualify as wars by any definition), and the Tamil uprising in Sri Lanka. The potential for highly unconventional future "wars" exists in areas such as the southern rim of successor states of the Soviet Union, larger parts of Africa, and southern Asia.

Although the list is tentative and probably incomplete, there are four characteristics of the new internal wars that differentiate them from conventional insurgencies. The first and most prominent characteristic is the apparent absence of clear military objectives that can be translated into coherent strategies and tactics. Unless the sheer terrorizing of populations or the maximum slaughter of fellow countrymen can be thought of as a military objective (flowing from what political objective?), it is difficult to decipher for what purpose fighting occurred in Sierre Leone. If it is to forcefully overcome the hostile ability of the government and its supporters to gain political power and institute a series of alternative policies, no one has articulated those policies or translated them into grand or, for that matter, battlefield strategy.

The new internal wars lack the sense of political and military orderliness that one associates with Cold War–era wars of national liberation that followed some variation of the Maoist mobile-guerrilla strategy. Whereas guerrilla warfare is inherently spontaneous in many of its acts, insurgent wars do generally conform to some observable strategic design. (In other words, what may seem chaotic in insurgent warfare at the platoon level makes much more sense at the level of grand strategy.)

This is hardly the case with many of the instances of new internal war. Rather, the new wars more closely conform to the description of the American Civil War by the Prussian observer Helmuth Karl von Moltke as "two armed mobs chasing one another across the countryside, from which nothing can be learned." Finding a strategic—or even tactical—rationale for the Somali "technicals" or the rampaging Hutu "militias" takes a stretch of the imagination.

The second characteristic involves the degree of irregularity of the forces. Insurgent forces are by their nature irregular in certain senses: They fight in different manners, are organized differently, and often do not wear military uniforms to help identify friend and foe. This is especially true of the warriors of the new internal wars.

The third characteristic of these wars is the absence of even an appearance of military order and discipline. Although the war-crimes process may reveal some hierarchy to have been present in Rwanda, the reportage of the slaughter made it appear that the militia units were little more than marauding bands acting quite independently of any order and showing no discipline whatsoever in the actions they were committing. The clansmen in Somalia showed little sense of military training and the discipline it entails, and the same can be said of the combatants in Haiti, Sierre Leone, and Liberia.

This lack of discipline manifests itself in the fourth characteristic: the level of ferocity and even atrocity that is routinely committed in these conflicts. Certainly, atrocious behavior in combat situations is not unknown even among the most highly trained and disciplined forces. In the American experience, for instance, one has only to point to acts against Vietnamese civilians in the latter stages of the war, when military discipline lagged and nervous conscripts intent only on surviving their tours tended to treat any Vietnamese as the enemy. The epitome of this was the slaughter at My Lai, although numerous similar incidents occurred on a smaller scale. The actions of the U.S.

Army against the plains Indians after the American Civil War also demonstrates that atrocious behavior belongs to no specific geographic or cultural distinction.

The scale and persistence of atrocious behavior in the new internal wars is nevertheless extreme. A distinguishing characteristic of these conflicts is the extent to which unarmed and otherwise innocent civilians are the major, if not sole, targets of the military campaigns being waged. The infamous detention camps and random acts of terror against the citizens of Sarajevo have defined the character of the war in Bosnia; standard military encounters between the armed forces of the combatting sides seems the exception. The "campaign" in Somalia was basically to starve civilians to death or into submission. Shining Path is waging a campaign of terror against the Peruvian people in which a prime means of control is the decapitation of recalcitrants (including, in some reported cases, sewing the heads back on—*backwards*). The Sudanese government, based on its infamous *fatwa,* endorses acts of murder against civilians by the armed forces on religious grounds (including unconfirmed reports of execution by crucifixion). Sierre Leone's RUF has conducted campaigns that routinely include murder, rape, and theft. Rwanda was nothing less than an instance of organized genocide. And the list goes on.

This pattern reveals complete ignorance of or disdain for the laws of war. Wars of the twentieth century have admittedly blurred traditional sanctions against systematic and purposive attacks on civilians. The Holocaust is the most obvious example of the twentieth century's regression from older standards of just war justly conducted, matched by the Nazi genocides in the Ukraine and elsewhere. It would be difficult to justify in traditional terms the systematic destruction of enemy cities, such as the firebombing of Tokyo and Dresden and the atomic bombing of Hiroshima and Nagasaki. It is almost certain, for instance, that such American leaders as General Curtis LeMay—who commanded the incineration of Tokyo—would have been treated as a war criminal had Japan won.)

If the discovery of mass graves containing innocent civilians has become a depressingly familiar part of the new landscape, it is quite obviously not an invention of the failed states of the Second Tier, and it would be condescending and probably racist for analysts of the First Tier to suggest otherwise. We all have too much blood on our own hands to be so disdainful of others.

Nonetheless, the atrocity is noteworthy, especially but not solely in those instances in which it is about the only form that "military activity" takes. A whole new industry of war-crimes trial has certainly opened up, although it is not clear that the system has the resources to try and punish the numerous war criminals. At the same time, the atrocities are much more public than they were in the past. Older atrocities (the Nazi death camps, for instance) were rumored but not directly observed until well after the ghoulish business was over. The Rwandan rampage, similar in content to some Western atrocities, was presented in its goriest detail only hours or days after it occurred. Such publicity makes atrocities more difficult to ignore, particularly because they are the visible blot on a generally improving international landscape.

CONCLUSIONS: DEALING WITH NEW INTERNAL WARS

Understanding the differences between the new and the more conventional war is important for determining how they can be ended and the extent to which the international system can participate in reconstructing failed states or creating viable states. A full exploration of systemic responses, and especially the limits of military intervention, is the central topic of the next chapter.

Even under the best of circumstances, reconstructing societies that have undergone civil conflicts is a difficult business. As Richard Haass notes, "The bitterness unleashed by civil wars tends to be hard to overcome." It is hard enough when the sides confine themselves to voluntary or self-interested restraints imposed by the need to appeal to common centers of gravity. When there is little or no sense of common social values and governance breaks down (weak society, weak state), then the floodgates of atrocity seem to open wide. The ensuing flood can only further embitter the parties and endanger the prospects for reconciliation.

In the "post–Cold War edition" of his *New Forces, Old Forces,* Seyom Brown offers the chilling prospect that Bosnia may be a harbinger of the future. His argument, in essence, is that if the conflict had occurred during the Cold War, one or the other side would have perceived sufficient interest to have prevented the war from breaking out in the first place or would have moved to stop it before it reached the levels it did.

Brown attributes the failure to act decisively in Bosnia to "strategic indifferen[ce]" on the part of the major powers. This principle is very close to the observation that those countries happen to be outside the growing prosperity of the emerging global economy. Will the genocidal flames in failed states be allowed to burn until all the fuel is used up while the system remains indifferent? Once again, the eventual outcome in Bosnia may provide the model. That war, like so many ongoing internal wars, had roots in long-held hatreds—namely the atrocities committed by and against Croats and Serbs in World War II, and Muslim collaboration during the Ottoman period. Recollections of those crimes helped to generate much of the fury that was unleashed when the Bosnian Muslims announced their independence.

Will Bosnia successfully reconstruct itself, even with the carefully drawn lines that separate many of the groups from one another? Neighbor will still look at neighbor and wonder if that person slaughtered a relative or a friend. The bitterness that led to war can only have been made worse by the atrocities that occurred on all sides. Yet the international system did finally come to the aid of Bosnia, and foreign troops are in place to keep the combatants apart, to facilitate the healing of wounds, to resolve the political details of partition, and even to assist in the physical and economic rebuilding of the country. Will other countries be so lucky?

Two major questions remain to be addressed. The first question is what the international system *can* do to affect the conduct of new internal wars. Chapter 5 assesses whether the experience of outside intervention in insurgencies carries over to new internal wars and whether effective actions are indeed possible, and examines the possible institutional and financial requirements of such efforts. The second question, which is the subject of Chapter 6, is what the international system *will* do if faced with a continuation of the pattern of new internal wars.

REFERENCES

Bell-Fialkoff, Andrew. "A Brief History of Ethnic Cleansing." *Foreign Affairs* 72, 3 (Summer 1993): 110–121.

Brown, Seyom. *New Forces, Old Forces and the Future of World Politics: Post–Cold War Edition.* New York: HarperCollins Publishers, 1995.

Damrosch, Lori Fisler, ed. *Enforcing Restraint: Collective Intervention in Internal Conflicts.* New York: Council on Foreign Relations Press, 1993.

Etzioni, Amatai. "The Evils of Self-Determination." *Foreign Policy* 89 (Winter 1992/93): 21–35.

Flint, Julie. "On the Wrong Side of a Jihad." *World Press Review,* November 1995: 37–38 (reprinted from *The Independent* of London).

Friedman, Thomas L. "The Next Rwanda." *New York Times* (national edition), January 26, 1996: A15.

Haass, Richard N. *Intervention: The Use of American Military Force in the Post–Cold War World.* Washington, D.C.: Carnegie Endowment Books, 1994.

Helman, Gerald B., and Steven R. Ratner. "Saving Failed States." *Foreign Policy* 89 (Winter 1992/93): 3–20.

Keegan, John. *A History of Warfare.* London: Hutchinson, 1993.

Krauthammer, Charles. "The Unipolar Moment." *Foreign Affairs* 70, 1 (1990/91): 23–33.

Project Ploughshares. *Armed Conflicts Report: Causes, Conflicting Parties, Negotiations.* Waterloo, Ont.: Institute of Peace and Conflict Studies, 1994.

Snow, Donald M., and Eugene Brown. *The Contours of Power: An Introduction to Contemporary International Relations.* New York: St. Martin's Press, 1996.

5

Systemic Responses

Along with economic and political development, the problem of violence in the countries of the Second Tier is the major international systemic problem, as well as a source of great concern between the tiers. The foci of *intertier* violence include terrorism and the possible use of weapons of mass destruction by Second Tier states against First Tier states. Sometimes the problems of intertier violence will be connected to new internal war; the wave of terrorist activity in France, for instance, is the result of Algerian fundamentalist attempts to force France to abandon support for the secular military government in Algeria. With the signal exception of the Scud missile attack during the Gulf War against a U.S. barracks in Dharan, Saudi Arabia, which killed twenty-seven Pennsylvania reservists, the problem of weapons proliferation fortunately remains theoretical.

The more prevalent problem is *intratier* violence within the Second Tier. Within the pattern of violence and stability in the post–Cold War international system, new internal war is the most important international security concern that confronts relations between the tiers.

In the Cold War, taking sides in internal wars was often justified (and even justifiable) on grounds of national security—the failure to prevent the overthrow of a friendly (e.g., anticommunist) government could upset balances of power and hence endanger national interests. With the Cold War in the past, such justifications have disappeared; in most cases, few if any residual national interests, traditionally considered, remain for most First Tier states in the outcomes of these wars. The exceptions are those conflicts that are physically proximate and annoying to First Tier states (Haitian refugees flooding Florida), those in which former colonial interests are involved (France and Algeria; the Russians and the "near abroad"), and those in which vital resources such as oil are involved (the Persian Gulf and more recently Azerbaijan).

Where none of these exceptions holds, any form of systemic response must be based on interests other than national. One such interest is international security: the idea that the peace and stability of the overall system is a shared value and interest. The promotion and expansion of the global economy to parts of the world excluded because of instability might be one justification for intervention. Another interest, and one raised frequently by Boutros-Ghali, has been so-called humanitarian, even vital humanitarian interests: defense of those basic human rights that, when grossly abused by governments or other groups within states, compel an international response. Interrupting campaigns of genocide within a state might justify intervention.

If the brief post–Cold War experience is any guide, the First Tier is ambivalent about the problem of Second Tier violence and its possible solutions. Early activism conditioned by an apparent success (liberating Kuwait) spawned further activism that turned sour (Somalia). The system did not respond (except for limited—and controversial—French interference) in Rwanda, and its path toward ending the Bosnian war was long and tortured at best. The First Tier currently shows little interest in the process of economic and political development that may lead to democratization and stability in the Second Tier. The problem is likely to worsen if some of the larger and more unstable countries such as India enter processes of disintegration, or if the epidemic of violence spreads more widely across Africa, a decidedly likely phenomenon. Second Tier governments, especially in the failed states, have shown little ability to control or eradicate movements against them. This is particularly appalling given the apparent ability of the criminal and narcotics insurgencies to sustain themselves without the outside assistance that was the mother's milk of Cold War–era insurgencies. These conflicts will be impossible to ignore, thanks to the growing reach of global media; anyone who missed the gory details of Rwanda on television could certainly find them in *Newsweek* or *Time,* for instance.

How the First Tier states choose to deal with Second Tier internal violence will be one of the defining characteristics of the new international system. Because no clear pattern has yet emerged, I will frame the options in broad terms that include the moral and political question of what *should* the international system do. I will include some of the structural forms that systemic responses might take, and examine the mechanics of possible intervention in light of traditional foreign intervention. The discussion will also include the different dynamics of what I call peace imposition and the ongoing problem of state building. The chapter ends with a look at that most tortured example of systemic response, the war in Bosnia and Herzegovina.

WHAT SHOULD AND CAN BE DONE?

The problems posed by new internal wars in the failed, failing, or potentially failing states of the world have not been systematically addressed; nor have viable solutions been devised. Much of the underlying structure of the problems is rooted in the decolonization process, as described in Chapter 2: desperately poor countries with little human or material infrastructure, unprepared in any meaningful way for self-governance. A comprehensive and effective response requires more than a sense of obligation on the part of the former colonizers and other states of the First Tier.

The basic structure of the problem (as I argue in the third edition of *National Security,* for instance) is that the excesses so often associated with new internal war exist at two distinct and often unconnected levels. The first and most obvious level involves some form of atrocious behavior, usually being inflicted on an apparently innocent civilian population and graphically presented on home television screens. Whether it is Kurds dying on Turkish mountains, starving Somali babies, maimed Rwandans, or gaunt, hollow-eyed Bosnians peering through the wire fences that imprison them, the images are heart-wrenching. One's first reaction is to reach out, to bring the suffering to an end. It is a noble instinct I call the "do something" syndrome.

Unfortunately, treating the symptoms does little to cure the underlying cause of the suffering. Getting the Kurds off the mountainsides and into protected areas stopped the dying, but it did not address the underlying issue: the relationship between the Iraqi government and its Kurdish population. Opening up supply routes to allow food to flow saved upwards of a hundred thousand Somalians (a U.S. government estimate used to justify the effort) from starvation but did not, and could not, address the anarchy in that country that caused the crisis in the first place. A genocidal rampage was the symptom in Rwanda; an inability to govern the country was the problem from which it arose.

The second level of the crisis is the inability of such states to govern themselves. This core problem creates the need for state building: the development of viable political structures that will be viewed as legitimate by the population of the country, and the education and training of politicians, civil servants, police, and a military force the citizens will trust and support. The absence of democratic structures, combined with wretched living conditions, causes states to fail in the first place. In Haiti, the military and the "police" (often little more than the old *ton ton macute* of the Duvalier days) ruled in a reign of terror. At its height, the Shining Path movement in Peru benefitted from the fact that government forces were often more brutal to the population than were the rebels. A similar situation apparently exists in Sierre Leone.

What Should Be Done?

Ideally, the citizens of the affected country will undertake the process of state building themselves, possibly with invisible or low-profile assistance from outsiders. In some cases this is feasible: The recovery of Peru under Albert Fujimori (admittedly aided by the suspension of much of the constitution) offers a ray of hope in a country long beset by internal mismanagement, corruption, and brutality. However, given Peru's history as an independent, sovereign state since 1821, it may not be able to serve as a role model for countries in places such as Africa. If adequate internal resources for state building do not exist, then it follows that such resources must be imported from the outside. In all likelihood they will not be available within kindred Second Tier states (no one would suggest sending Liberians into Sierre Leone or vice versa, for instance) and will almost inevitably have to be provided by countries of the First Tier.

If state building is to follow internal war, then it must involve a military commitment. Forces called in to end any suffering will probably need to stay on to guarantee that the fighting does not break out again, providing a shield behind which the state-building process can commence and progress. The military role is necessary but secondary to the political process of developing government structures and personnel to guard the country against another outbreak of violence. This process requires great skill and patience on the part of both the government and the intervenor.

This fundamental point is often overlooked or underemphasized in discussions of what can and should be done. There is a basic divide between efforts to alleviate the worst symptoms and attacking underlying causes. The first effort can normally be accomplished fairly easily, as in reinstating the supply of food in Somalia. The trouble is that this effort does little to attack the greater underlying problem, which is the creation of a legitimate state. That problem is difficult and requires a fundamentally different, long-term commitment that will inevitably alienate members of the indigenous population benefitting from the chaos and will likely have consequences (casualties, for instance) unacceptable to the American people. We leaped the divide by undertaking to disarm rival factions in Somalia with absolutely predictable results. In retrospect, we utterly missed the point by grousing about "mission creep" there when we instead had taken a mission "leap."

For a government to request or tolerate outside interference in the first place is something of an admission of failure, and the greater the need for outside help (as manifested by large and growing numbers of outsiders), the weaker the regime is likely to appear. The intervention is also likely to become more unpopular the longer it lasts: the intervenors will be resented by the natives if they are perceived as an occupying and possibly even recolonizing force (especially if the "invaders" are disdainful of local ways of doing things). As ingratitude becomes public, public opinion in the country providing the assistance is likely to weaken. Moreover, the slow pace of progress is almost certain to result in a continuing sense of frustration on all sides.

The "do something" syndrome provides a powerful drive to alleviate suffering and deprivation. The desire to help is certainly noble, but interference in internal wars is not always morally justified. One may be interrupting entirely normal developmental processes that would work themselves out as well or better if left to their natural progression. This is not, of course, much solace to those who are undergoing the horrors and whose misery is extended by outside inaction. Almost all societies that have gone through the development process have dark moments in their histories. In the United States, for instance, some of the campaigns to capture the western territories from the native American Indians (Fenneman's massacre in eastern Colorado; Wounded Knee) would look about as bad on television as the atrocities committed in the name of some contemporary version of manifest destiny. Nevertheless, the process of transforming the United States into a modern continental power required that the native population be either removed or subjugated. Had there been UN missions or the like at that time to protect the Ogallala Sioux or the Apache nation, the process might have been slower (and conceivably better for the Indians). On the other hand, this might simply have prolonged the agony and further embittered relations. Outside intervention requires a careful balance between moral outrage at atrocity and prudent consideration of the most effective course of action.

What Can Be Done, and by Whom?

There are considerable practical limitations to what the countries of the First Tier are likely to do about suffering induced by internal war in the Second Tier. Some of these limits arise from the structure of the military situation, which is the focus of the next section. Some of them arise from disinterest on the part of First World countries, and on the resources that can reasonably be brought to bear, given competing priorities and the large number of actual and potential applications.

To explain these limitations involves a twofold approach. The first step is to lay out a model of what can happen when outsiders seek to interfere in internal crises. It is principally derived from my observation of the effort in Somalia, and thus should be thought of as a "worst-case" model. The second step is to consider which countries or institutions are best suited to mount and coordinate such efforts.

The worst-case model is depicted in Figure 5.1 as a ten-step, circular process.

Figure 5.1
Internal War Cycle

1. Crisis forms
2. NGOs, others arrive
3. Crisis worsens
4. Crisis explodes
5. Outsider intervenes
6. Outsider faces dilemma
7. Outsider is frustrated
8. Outsider becomes disillusioned
9. Outsider withdraws
10. Crisis reforms/ returns

Somalia and the Internal War Cycle

The cycle begins with the formation of a crisis. Normally there is some warning that a serious problem is imminent. In a phenomenon not unlike the democratic contradiction regarding counterinsurgency, the signals may be ignored or undervalued until the crisis reaches critical proportions. In the case of the impending crisis in Burundi in early 1996, Canadian sources apparently intercepted a large number of messages from Rwanda that, if put together, would have suggested that the Hutu rampage was going to occur. In Somalia, Jeffrey Clark and Chester Crocker, while disagreeing on the success of the overall mission, agree that UNISOM I, the negotiating mission before "peacekeepers" entered the country, "collapsed from bureaucratic infighting and an inability to provide safety for relief operations," in Crocker's words. Haiti's President Aristide languished for three years in exile before the United States negotiated his return in 1994.

As crises mount, the second phase begins with the arrival of outsiders. These take the form of intergovernmental organizations (IGOs), of which the United Nations is the most prominent example, and nongovernmental organizations (NGOs), including both those who provide humanitarian relief (such as CARE, the International Red Cross, and Doctors Without Borders) and those who monitor human rights (such as Amnesty International and Human Rights Watch). The crisis worsens (for instance, the more persistent interruptions in the provision of food and health care in Somalia).

In the third phase, the situation progressively worsens and the frustration increases on all sides, but especially within the IGOs and NGOs. In Somalia, the UNISOM I diplomatic mission's attempt to negotiate a settlement among the warring clans failed entirely, and the food givers and health providers were increasingly frustrated. From their vantage point, it was difficult to understand why anyone would interfere with the lofty purpose of saving human lives. From the vantage point of the warring clans, the NGOs were simply getting in the way of attempts to force their enemies into submission.

In phase four, the deteriorating situation eventually causes the situation to explode into the public eye. In the case of Somalia, this more or less coincided with the collapse of the UNISOM I mission in early December 1992. The media had become aware of the widespread suffering and the potential for starvation; television screens, magazine covers, and the front pages of newspapers were filled with images of the distended bellies and sunken eyes of pitiful Somali children. The American public, including its recently defeated political leadership, was horrified; the "do something" syndrome was activated.

On December 4, 1992, President Bush, after consulting briefly with President-elect Clinton, announced his intention to intervene and stop the suffering, acting through the UN and with multilateral backing. The result was armed intervention under the banner of the United Nations Task Force (UNITAF). U.S. Marines, accompanied by other foreign troops, landed at Mogadishu and elsewhere, quickly restored order, began reopening the transportation system so the food could flow, and provided a shield for the provision of humanitarian relief by NGOs and others. The symptom was attacked.

This phase was remarkably successful, which should have come as a surprise to absolutely no one. The impressive show of force by the heavily armed American-led troops simply intimidated the marauding clan-based gangs, who retreated in the same manner that guerrillas avoid overwhelmingly unfavorable situations. This was a case of the first phase of counterinsurgency, a large-unit show of force (at which, of course, the United States is best). Unfortunately, the success of this first stage is irrelevant to overall success in counterinsurgency, and although it was useful in Somalia, it could not address the real problem of anarchy. The solution to that problem was state building, the far more arduous task that parallels the second phase of counterinsurgency, when the action returns to the task of political conversion.

The apparent success of the fifth phase quickly gives way to the dilemma of the outsider: placing blame for the emergency in the first place and beginning the process of reconciliation among the parties. In Somalia this process began during the remainder of the UNITAF phase, which ended in April 1993 when American and other major-power forces withdrew from Somalia. While the Americans were there, things appeared to go well. The immediate crisis was overcome, and relations between the Americans and the most powerful clan leaders, such as Muhammed Farah Aidid, were cordial and encouraging. They were also misleading, because ultimate success required the "mission leap" to state building.

The appearance of progress during this phase had at least three elements. First, the American presence was adequately overwhelming that no one was going to risk attacking the U.S. troops for fear of retaliation. Second, this was also a period in which particularly Aidid, as the clan leader who controlled most of Mogadishu (where the Americans were most prominent) was courting the Americans in the hopes that they could be enlisted to (perhaps unwittingly) support his aspiration to emerge as the leader of the country. Third, and most important, there was no attempt at this time to begin the serious process of state building, which would inevitably disadvantage some or all factions and prompt their opposition and resistance. Treating the symptom while ignoring the underlying malaise created the illusion that the problem was being solved.

When UNITAF ended, the situation rapidly returned to its usual chaos. The remaining peacekeepers (especially the Pakistanis) were the subjects of violent attacks as the clan militias returned to the struggle for power. This in turn triggered phase seven, which was a frustrated reaction that involved the return of the Americans and others under the guise of UNISOM II in May 1993. (It is not always the case that leaving and returning will trigger this phase.) At this point the mission turned to state building, which would have been the original objective if the peacekeepers had been serious about ending the real crisis in Somalia—anarchy. That this was a serious change in direction (with equally serious military consequences that are discussed in the next section) was apparently not widely appreciated at the time, and it may not be universally understood today.

A quotation from Crocker (the chief African expert in the Bush State Department) illustrates the fuzziness of understanding: "As the initial intervention unfolded, Somalia was transformed from a famine-stricken backwater where heartless warlords and hopped-up teenage gangs reigned over helpless innocents into a laboratory for new theories of U.N. peacekeeping. Perhaps, ironically, the impressive leadership, coherence, and success of the U.S.-led UNITAF phase made it look too easy, facilitating the 'mission creep' that produced UNISOM II's vast nation-building mandate."

Given such an analysis, it is hardly surprising that UNISOM II experienced frustration. The flash point of the state-building mandate turned out to be the disarming of clan factions as the preface to creating a tranquil order. Many in the U.S. military understood the consequences of doing this and objected but were overruled. When UN/U.S. forces began the disarmament process, they effectively became partisan, in opposition to those whose power was diminished by the loss of their guns. When the Americans, operating out of Mogadishu, sought as part of their mission to disarm the fighters loyal to Aidid, they became part of Aidid's problem and he resisted. The result was a noticeable lack of progress and the increasing ingratitude of the citizens of Mogadishu who were also supporters of Aidid.

Crocker discusses UNISOM II as having had two distinct periods, and these conform rather closely to phases eight and nine of the cycle. Phase eight, in which the outsider (in this case, primarily the United States) becomes disillusioned, roughly conforms to the first period of UNISOM II, which he dates from May to October 1993. During this period there was a progressive public disillusionment in the United States with the entire operation, triggered by the rather obvious lack of progress in, among other things, bringing Aidid to justice for alleged crimes against the peacekeepers. This phase, and the first period of UNISOM II, ended with the counterattack by forces loyal to Aidid against American Rangers who had raided an alleged meeting in a hotel at which Aidid was said to be present. Eighteen Americans were killed, and imprinted on the public consciousness was the image of the corpse of one of the Americans being dragged through the dusty streets of Mogadishu. At that time, the fate of American participation was sealed, and the movement to phase nine began; at the same time, serious efforts toward state building were abandoned as UNISOM II moved to, in Crocker's words, "a scaled-back, accommodative phase."

Phase nine consisted of the final withdrawal of American forces. Shortly after the October 1993 Ranger incident, the Clinton administration announced that it would begin a phased drawdown of Americans in the UN command, who would be replaced by soldiers from other countries. The process was completed on March 25, 1994, when the last American peacekeepers departed, leaving a contingent of only fifty American soldiers to protect the diplomatic mission and a dozen to provide logistics support to the UN. In all, thirty American servicemen had been killed and 175 wounded. For practical purposes, the United States had washed its hands of the whole affair. The two principal clan leaders, Aidid and Ali Mahdi, signed a ceasefire agreement in Nairobi, Kenya, renouncing the use of violence.

The situation then turned to phase ten, in which the crisis could reignite. Nineteen thousand troops committed to the UN remained after the American withdrawal, but that number gradually decreased, and UNISOM II ended in March 1995 when the last UN troops departed. Left behind, of course, were the NGO relief workers now operating without the shield of UN peacekeepers. The clan-based factions remain. There is nothing resembling a national government in place; the future is nearly as uncertain as it was when Siad Barre was removed from power.

The Lessons of Somalia

Applying to the cycle of internal war the problem of Somalia allows for some interesting observations, especially for the comparison between intervention in new internal wars and intervention in conventional insurgency-counterinsurgency. The principal observation can be stated in a paradox that describes the multinational involvement in Somalia. It is quite clear from that experience that outsiders can be reasonably effective in dealing with these situations as long as they attack the symptom of the problem but avoid the root cause from which the symptom arose. It is equally clear that attempts to solve the underlying problems (and lessen the likelihood that the symptom will recur) are unlikely to be effective. Either way, one has come no closer to understanding why failed states fail.

The official assessment of Somalia (as reflected in the Crocker apologia) reflects the muddled thinking surrounding this question. The official line is that the mission was a success because it prevented the starvation of many people by mounting Operation Restore Hope. By this reasoning, the expansion of the mission to include state building was a mistake that should have been avoided. This comes very close to saying that outsiders should never undertake actions that might actually be worthwhile.

Outside forces need to get a better handle on what they are and are not willing to try to accomplish *before* commissioning any more Operation Restore Hopes. If the goal is the limited one of temporarily alleviating a bad situation in hope that it will heal itself once the wound is bound, then let them act accordingly and not veer from the purpose. The problem with this approach, of course, is that initial satisfaction with the results is likely to fade if the situation reverts. If, on the other hand, the goal is to attack the root cause and attempt to engage in state building (which *is* the problem in a number of the states undergoing new internal wars), then policymakers need to be up front about the difficulties that the commitment entails—no more whining about mission creep. They must also admit that the task may not be successful.

The core question is whether outside forces can do another country's state building for it. One response is that if it is abundantly clear that the state itself cannot accomplish the task, it will need outside assistance. This, however, raises several problems. First, it is not certain that the United States, the UN, or any other body has an effective blueprint for the task; dropping off sample copies of democratic constitutions and training the local police to be honest is a start, but it is not the complete answer. Second, there are inherent limitations on the leverage an intervening state has over the country in which it intervenes. This is a lesson from the counterinsurgency experience, but the dynamic may be a little different here. The more time a supporter of the counterinsurgency invests, the harder it is to cut those losses and leave (which the client will figure out). In state building, on the other hand, one can think of a public-opinion clock ticking from the beginning of the intervention that will inevitably run out; those in opposition simply have to wait out the process.

Third, even the most principled and fair-minded approach to state building is going to produce political winners and losers. The winners may support the efforts because they are advantaged, but the losers will eventually come to oppose their "benefactors." It is impossible not to become part of the partisan battle (just as it is impossible in peace-enforcement operations to remain neutral, a major point in the next section). Fourth, state building is a long and arduous business, and the longer the mission lasts, the more likely it is to be viewed, once again in Crocker's words, as "a modern version of trusteeship over an ex-colonial territory." Those being helped are likely to suspect the intentions of their benefactors, and to show a lack of gratitude for the effort.

Is this Somalia-based cycle the model for future engagement possibilities? It is hard to imagine another instance of a large intervention followed by a premature withdrawal, followed by the reinsertion of forces because the original accomplishment was unraveling due to inattention to the root cause. Nevertheless, the general dynamics of intervention, in a manner very similar to the Somalia experience, are almost certain to recur. State builders are going to be frustrated in their efforts, viewed by some as interlopers rather than as liberators, and opposed by some they seek to uplift. Moreover, the longer their efforts continue, the more pressure there will likely be for them to return home before the mission is accomplished. One may argue that the framework is too defeatist, even cynical. After all, the Haitian experience demonstrates that not all these things need occur; nevertheless, the book on successful Haitian statehood is hardly closed. Bosnia after the scheduled withdrawal of IFOR raises similar questions.

Who Takes the Lead?

The other concern raised at the beginning of this section was who should authorize and conduct these kinds of operations. There would appear to be four possible categories of interventions. The first are actions authorized and controlled by the UN. The ultimate form for such an operation would be a standing UN force, as suggested in Chapter VII of its charter. The second option would be an action authorized by the UN, which would then "deputize" either a regional organization or an individual state to carry out the mandate, with some UN consultative or regulatory presence. The third option would be for local regional organizations to mount and conduct operations on their own. The fourth option is for individual states, presumably with special interests of some kind, to act unilaterally.

Either UN option suffers from the ambivalence of members of the international community toward the world body. Such mood swings are captured in reviews of the UN's fiftieth anniversary (several of which are listed in the references). Buoyed by the apparent success of the Persian Gulf War to produce a UN-led new world order, the world organization became the agency of choice in 1992 and 1993, when ten new peacekeeping missions were authorized. That ardor faded noticeably in 1994 (with only two new missions), and even further in 1995 (with no new missions).

UN operations are compromised by two factors. The first is the well-publicized, perpetual financial crisis of the organization. This does not affect the authorization of missions (passing resolutions is cheap enough), but it does affect their implementation: States must make voluntary or involuntary contributions to underwrite UN activities. The organization is seriously limited when confronted with a country like the United States under Reagan, who simply refused to pay the national share for missions of which he disapproved. The UN reports that as of October 1995, members were well over $2 billion in arrears to the organization. Over three-quarters of that total covered peacekeeping assessments; the United States was by far the biggest debtor with a bill of $1.255 billion (Russia coming in second with a $497 million bill, all for peacekeeping).

The second problem is the UN's attitude and lack of expertise in conducting military matters. There are no reliable studies of which I am aware that document this, but there is a good deal of anecdotal evidence suggesting that most UN employees who, after all, join the organization to pursue world peace, are simply not equipped to direct military efforts. This is more a problem in active military operations than in traditional peacekeeping, but it is a concern nonetheless. The reluctance of UN officials to think in military terms may help explain why they characterize situations in peacekeeping terms when peacekeepers are inappropriate, such as in Somalia and Bosnia (UNPROFOR).

The second category is that of the UN deputizing either regional organizations or individual states to conduct missions intended to keep or create a peace. There is precedent for both. The actions against Bosnian Serbs (principally air strikes) during 1995 in retaliation for attacks against UN-designated safe havens were effectively "contracted" to NATO; and the enlarged peacekeeping force (IFOR) monitoring the Paris peace agreement is under NATO control. The American action in Haiti represents the deputizing of an individual country by the UN (though the operation was extended to the Organization of American States when American forces were withdrawn in 1995).

"Farming out" operational responsibility has both advantages and disadvantages. On the positive side, an organization such as

NATO has considerable practice at organizing and conducting military operations based on training, exercising, and limited insertion of forces into combat or humanitarian situations. One can reasonably expect the military side of a UN operation employing NATO-directed forces to operate effectively; certainly, the joint operations by Britain, France, and the United States in the Gulf War were facilitated by their NATO experience. It is not clear, however, that this advantage extends to other regional organizations.

A prominent disadvantage to the use of regional organizations is that there are not operational regional organizations in all the areas where they might be needed. The Organization of American States (OAS) is as close to a functioning regional organization as exists, but its operational area is relatively tranquil. There is no regional organization that covers South and Southeast Asia. The former Soviet Union has the Commonwealth of Independent States (CIS) as a putative security organization, but it exists more on paper than in fact and is dominated by Russia. Africa has the Organization of African Unity (OAU), but it has been remarkably ineffective. This demonstrates, in William Durch's terms, "the rudimentary level of development of regional security organizations" that reflects their "limited capabilities" in enforcing the peace. Moreover, it is not clear that peacekeeping forces composed exclusively of regional actors could be assembled that would meet the criteria of objectivity and neutrality, characteristics absolutely vital to success. Moreover, there has been insufficient experience in using regional organizations in this manner to know what the relationship between the regional organization and the UN would be in terms of reporting, direction, oversight, and the like, nor what financial arrangements would have to be made.

Individual states or regional organizations acting on their own are even less likely to be satisfactory. The problem of vested interests becomes even greater than with UN imprimatur; for example, India's incursion into Sri Lanka to dampen the Tamil Tiger uprising, and Russia's involvement in Georgia (technically a CIS action), which resulted in Georgia's joining the CIS, will almost certainly be viewed with suspicion. Organizations such as the OAU simply do not have the organizational, military, or financial wherewithal for these kinds of involvements.

There is no single, ideal organization for authorizing and conducting interventions into internal wars. Although the UN has absolutely no superior standing in international law that makes it a more legitimate body than any other (a point made strongly by Ernest Lefever), it has developed a certain authority as the most likely place to debate and authorize actions. The principal problem the UN faces is financial, and the problem has two distinct aspects.

The first aspect is the dependence of the world body on the large states, who are the only ones with the money and the forces to provide for any major involvement in internal wars. This is especially true of the United States, which has an effective triple veto over UN operations. It has the formal veto in the Security Council, of course, but any sizable UN operation requires American peacekeeping contributions (which it is capable of withholding) and the provision of American logistical support to transport and sustain UN forces. The refusal of the United States to provide either can doom an operation from the start and thus serve as an effective veto.

The other part of the financial limitation is on the kinds of operations that the UN can sponsor. Traditional UN peacekeeping operations have the advantage of being relatively inexpensive; the forces are modest in number, lightly equipped, and relatively stationary in deployment. There is an implicit preference for peacekeeping among UN officials as a form of activism they can afford. Sending forces into combat zones—into ongoing internal wars—is a much more strenuous and expensive proposition. Such operations rapidly exceed the financial resources of the UN unless assessments and contributions are increased dramatically (which is unlikely). Yet these other forms of activity are those more obviously called for in response to the new internal war.

THE OPERATIONAL LEVEL

The language of peacekeeping has dominated the discussion of how to respond to new internal wars because it has taken place within the framework of UN actions. The result has been a set of distinctions that is inappropriate to the actual situations in which action may be contemplated (which much more closely resemble outside intervention on behalf of counterinsurgencies). There is a misapprehension of the different operational environments and mission problems that intervention forces will encounter. This was the case in Somalia: Peacekeepers were dispatched into a situation in which peace did not truly exist. They were tolerated as long as they kept to the traditional peacekeeper's role (supervising the relief effort), but when they began the more arduous task of making a peace and creating a state, they entered a combat zone. The confusion is epitomized by the tragic case of UNPROFOR in Bosnia, where a classic peacekeeping force was thrown into a full-scale war and became the pawn and whipping boy of the combatants.

This section seeks to overcome the confusing distinctions that have become the parameters for discussing different solutions to new internal wars; to distinguish the various operational environments and mission challenges that forces may encounter; and to examine how American policy has evolved in this light.

Definitional Distinctions

The definitional confusion about systemic responses to new internal wars has its genesis in 1991 and 1992. Encouraged by the positive experience of the Gulf War, the UN Security Council commissioned Secretary-General Boutros-Ghali to produce a report on world security problems and possible UN responses. The result, *An Agenda for Peace,* was published in 1992; its taxonomy of possible actions became the standard for future discussions and was, for better or worse, picked up in its entirety by the U.S. Army, (attaching slightly different meanings to one of the categories). This classification of five forms of action, to which I have added the stage of conflict in which each might be contemplated, is depicted in Table 5.1.

Table 5.1 Action Options and Conflict Stages

Policy Option	Conflict Stage
Preventive diplomacy	Prewar
Peacemaking	Wartime
Peace enforcement	
Peacekeeping	Postwar
Peace building	

The list reflects traditional UN roles and missions but also adds less-conventional roles. The unexceptional roles are those played when hostilities are not active. *Preventive diplomacy,* according to the report, refers to "actions to prevent existing disputes from escalating into conflicts, and to limit the spread of the latter when they occur." *Peacekeeping* refers to the conventional role of interposing forces between formerly warring factions to prevent them from coming into contact and running the risk of reopening hostilities. This physical separation is expected to cool emotion and facilitate the peace process, but that is not always the case; the UNFICYP mission to Cyprus has been in place since 1964 and serves to allow two communities to coexist on the island with no apparent incentive to settle their differences. *Peace building* refers to "actions to identify and support structures which will tend to strengthen and solidify peace in order to avoid a relapse into conflict." Peace building, in other words, is something akin to state building.

There is nothing particularly controversial about these three designations, and one can cite examples of each. The Oakley mission to Somalia is an example of attempted preventive diplomacy, even if it failed in the long run. There are numerous historical and ongoing examples of peacekeeping: The UN Emergency Force (UNEF) along the border between Israel and Egypt in the Sinai between 1956 and 1967 served as a prototype, and something like peace building was the avowed purpose of American military and civilian personnel in Haiti during 1994 and 1995.

The conceptual distinctions unravel when one turns to activities undertaken during wartime (although Boutros-Ghali does not make an explicit distinction between peacetime and wartime when laying out his terms). *Peacemaking* refers to "peaceful means" of bringing warring parties together to cease fighting by taking actions authorized under Chapter VI of the UN Charter. Presumably, the Owens-Vance mission to Bosnia, followed by the imposition of economic sanctions against Serbia, qualify as peacemaking efforts, as did the American-sponsored peace negotiations in late 1995. *Peace enforcement* refers to efforts by deputized forces under UN control to reestablish a lapsed peace. The reinsertion of UN (including U.S.) troops into Somalia under the banner of UNISOM II was probably a peace-enforcement mission.

These five activities are presented as a kind of logical continuum: When trouble is brewing, you dispatch the diplomats to engage in preventive diplomacy and avoid war. If that effort fails, then you begin the process of negotiating peace, up to and including threatening sanctions (peacemaking). When the negotiators succeed, then one calls in peacekeepers to enforce the cease fire while reconciliatory talks proceed. Should there be a breach of the peace, then peace enforcement must be undertaken. Once peace is reinforced, then it can be solidified by peace building.

There are at least three things wrong with this neatly constructed framework. The first is that the suggestion of continuity is misleading. Laying out the concepts as a logical progression creates the false impression that movement through the stages is a process of equal (or at least parallel) steps. Continuity holds for three activities (preventive diplomacy, peacemaking, and peace building) in the sense that they are all diplomatic and political activities. One can make the case that peacekeeping also fits into the line of parallel actions because, although military force is present, its role is both restrained and restraining.

The movement to peace enforcement, even within the limited definition provided, involves the insertion of active fighting forces to reinstate peace. This implies that the forces so inserted have, at least potentially, a fighting role. (The U.S. Army's adaptation of the peace-enforcement term does admit a range of potentially lethal possibilities.) The decision to insert fighting forces represents a *qualitative* change in a UN mission; this difference was dramatically demonstrated when UNISOM made the mission leap of engaging in state building. One could even argue that peace building, when it is opposed by some or all parties, represents a qualitative discontinuity from the other actions.

The second problem is the counterintuitive, distorting language used to describe these various actions. The problem lies in the terms used to describe action when fighting is going. Peacemaking, for instance, is an orthodox term used to describe a wide array of actions in which instruments of power are used to make fighting stop. The distortion is the implication that peacemaking is limited to nonviolent methods (those authorized under Chapter VI of the charter) rather than lethal methods (such as those employed under Chapter VII to evict Iraq from Kuwait).

The distortion is even more striking in the use of the term peace enforcement. According to conventional use of the English language, peacekeeping and peace enforcement should be roughly the same thing; the enforcement of peace, after all, logically presumes the existence of a peace to be enforced. Boutros-Ghali's classification uses the term to describe the remedy of a breached peace. The U.S. Army only compounds the confusion by referring in its doctrinal manuals to peace enforcement as a subcategory of "operations other than war" or even "peace operations."

The third, and most damning, problem of the classification is that it is incomplete and hence inapplicable to the most important situations to which it should be applied. Of the five categories listed, only one mentions the possibility of actively employing force as a means to end a war, and that use is limited to reinstating a breached peace. What is glaringly omitted is the active use of military force to create peace between two warring parties. In normal use, peacemaking would serve that purpose, but the Boutros-Ghali taxonomy limits the meaning to nonlethal activities. An additional concept is needed to complete the idea. *Peace creation* might serve in this regard, although I find it an unnecessarily soft term (military force rarely being creative). More descriptive, if harsher, is *peace imposition,* the coercive use of military force by outside parties to force warring parties to cease their hostile, lethal actions toward one another.

Peace Imposition

The term peace imposition is a necessary addition to the classification because it applies to numerous situations in which the system may contemplate taking action. The Boutros-Ghali taxonomy is utterly inadequate to describe the actions that might have been taken in Bosnia to end that war between 1992 and the end of 1995; if there was to be peace, it had to have been imposed. The same is true for Somalia in 1992 and 1993, and Haiti in 1994; it would be true today should action be required to restore (or create) order in such places as Perú, Sierre Leone, Sri Lanka, or Tajikistan. The limiting options contained in the Boutros-Ghali formulation simply do not apply to the most difficult situations that the new internal wars create.

The Boutros-Ghali framework suggests deceptively simple solutions that do not reflect a broad divide between peacekeeping and its related complex of activities, peace imposition/state building. The actions included in the taxonomy are reasonable responses to situations in which the parties are not in fundamental, life-and-death disagreement and on which rational processes of conflict resolution can be brought to bear. The problem is that the new internal wars often do not fit or even approximate such a description; they are often marked by enormous savagery of military conduct and incoherence of political purpose. Preventive diplomacy did not work in Sierre Leone, when the Revolutionary United Front had absolutely no interest in ending a warlike chaos that permits it to loot the land. That "insurgency" will not end until someone puts the RUF out of business. Similarly, the government-sponsored slaughter of infidels in Sudan will not be ended by appeals to reason; it will end only if the Sudanese government is forced to stop the killing.

The term *peace imposition* implies a very difficult business, with strong parallels to the dynamics of intervention by outsiders in insurgency-counterinsurgency situations. The language of peacekeeping was used in Somalia, and the operation was designed according to the spirit of the Boutros-Ghali taxonomy. But the analogy was false:

Somalia was a war zone, and the only way to change that situation was to go to war with the fighting parties and force them to stop—in other words, to impose peace.

Environments and Characteristics of Peacekeeping and Peace Imposition

Although I acknowledge that there is a difference between peacekeeping and what is erroneously called peace enforcement, from this point I will use the more descriptive term peace imposition exclusively. The intellectual and professional communities have been remarkably slow to recognize this distinction, but it is critical to understanding why outside interventions in peacekeeping situations are often successful and why intervention in places requiring peace imposition will almost always fail.

There is some recognition that the new internal wars are different from those of the Cold War. Leslie Gelb, for instance, describes this relatively new phenomenon in terms of "wars of national debilitation, a steady run of uncivil civil wars sundering fragile but functioning nation-states and gnawing at the well-being of stable nations." He suggests caution in approaching these conflicts but does not advocate a policy. From the operational, professional side of the house, *Armed Forces Journal International* picks up the cudgel but grasps it incorrectly. Its October 1995 issue has an article entitled "Combat Peacekeeping," demonstrating a remarkable ability to blur basic distinctions. Its November 1995 issue goes a step farther by suggesting the need for "creating a peace to keep"—imposing a peace that can then be turned over to peacekeepers. Such reasoning is dangerous and can lead the United States and anyone else who accepts it into problems that would make the Vietnam War experience look simple. The fact is that the environments in which the two activities are conducted are fundamentally different.

Peacekeeping

Peacekeeping, in its conventional sense, occurs within its own special set of circumstances. The most fundamental condition is that peace exists between the parties following the conclusion of hostilities. Examples include the various missions to monitor ceasefires between Israel and its neighbors and to monitor the peace between India and Pakistan. The classic method of peacekeepers is to interpose themselves between the recently warring parties to keep them apart.

The success of a true peacekeeping mission requires that all parties want the peacekeepers there because they all prefer the absence of war to its continuation or resumption. Peacekeepers are not resented on the grounds that they tip the scales in favor of one faction (or state) or the other—the postwar balance has already been set, and it is the role of the peacekeeper to reinforce that agreement. In such circumstances cooperation between the peacekeeper and the formerly warring parties is likely. Presumably, there is a will among the parties to reach a political solution or at least the mutual desire to avoid a return to war, and the peacekeepers' contribution to that end is recognized and appreciated by all parties.

The mission requirements for peacekeepers are relatively simple and straightforward. The primary requirement is that peacekeepers remain neutral, thereby ensuring the support and trust of the former adversaries whose postwar behavior they are monitoring. Traditionally, this has meant drawing forces from neutral countries or small states that do not pose any military threat, and especially from states such as Norway and Canada that have specially earmarked and trained units designated for peacekeeping duty. Peacekeepers, in effect, serve as honest brokers in the postwar process, and they are likely to remain effective as long as two conditions hold: their neutrality is maintained, and none of the parties attempts to change the political outcome by force (the situation for which Boutros-Ghali prescribes peace enforcers).

This limited role also defines the operational requirements of peacekeepers. Because their role is observation and physical interposition, they need not be prepared or equipped for physical combat. They need only small, defensive weapons (traditionally only for use in personal self-defense), and they do not need to be sent in large numbers, therefore they are relatively inexpensive to transport and sustain. This helps explain why the UN, given its very limited resources, likes to think all missions can be handled in this manner.

When a mission's environment does not meet these criteria, *it is not a peacekeeping situation.* To describe it in peacekeeping terms distorts reality and can form the basis for wrongheaded and even tragic consequences. UNPROFOR's mission, for instance, could only be described as peacekeeping during the very first days in which it was interposed to monitor a Serb-Croat ceasefire that rapidly dissolved. Continuing to refer to and configure it as a peacekeeping force made it ineffective, even irrelevant to the situation on the ground. The same was true of UNISOM when it took up the state-building mission (which was necessary if it was truly to solve the problem at hand).

Peace Imposition

Peace imposition operates in an entirely different environment that is much more akin to the dynamics of outside intervention in civil war. At its most obvious level, the difference is between a condition of peace and a condition of war; peace imposers enter war zones for the purpose of causing military hostilities to cease. In such circumstances, at least one (and possibly all) of the competing parties prefer the continuation of hostilities to peace; otherwise they would have created a peace themselves, in which case peacekeepers would be the appropriate response. One party may prefer to continue the war because it is winning and wishes to win more, or because it is losing and hopes to recoup some of its losses. The satisfaction of one side at ending hostilities at any point will correspond to the dissatisfaction of the other side at any point. This fundamental dynamic explains why almost any outcome of the peace process over Bosnia conducted in Dayton, Ohio, was to be viewed as suspect: It was difficult to imagine all three sides being satisfied with any territorial settlement.

The result is that peace imposers will inevitably be resented and opposed by some or all of the warring factions. Their role is like that of the police officer breaking up a drunken brawl in a bar: Ending the fighting may be to the greater good of the brawlers and certainly of the uninvolved clientele and the management; the problem is convincing the drunks of this at the time. By analogy, innocent victims within the country and the international community may applaud the insertion of peace imposers in internal war; the problem is convincing the warring parties of the value of the service.

The practical outcome of this dynamic is that peace imposers are going to be opposed, probably eventually militarily, and they are going to be unappreciated by at least some factions within the countries to which they are committed. The resentment and potential for opposition may not initially be appreciated by the peace imposers. Normally, at least in the post–Cold War involvements, they enter war zones with overwhelming force that intimidates the parties and causes the appearance of tranquillity that belies their longer-term impact on the underlying problem. No one initially opposed the American landing in Somalia, and U.S. forces left Haiti before opposition could congeal. Faced with the robust force that is often used (in keeping with the Colin Powell–inspired doctrine of overwhelming force), the opponents lie low, knowing they cannot successfully confront the outsiders on the battlefield. Instead, common sense suggests trying to co-opt the outsiders, and if that fails, waiting them out until they leave. If *that* fails, then confrontation can occur. Certainly, that was the dynamic in Somalia for the Americans, and IFOR's early experience reinforces the point.

The operational effect of these dynamics is that the forces used for peace imposition must be combat troops equipped to perform offensive missions with heavy equipment and large contingents. Such forces will inevitably be more expensive than peacekeeping forces, and they will almost certainly incur politically unpopular casualties. Although peace imposers will almost always enter these situations with high-minded notions of neutrality and fairness, their intervention will be regarded as partisan by whomever ends up with the short end of the stick.

These dynamics are virtually identical to those in Vietnam. The United States was, of course, partisan from the beginning (which is the major difference), but it entered to end an insurgency. It succeeded wildly at first (when the Viet Cong and North Vietnamese had entered the third stage of mobile-guerrilla warfare in 1965), but after this the enemy hunkered down for protracted opposition. Eventually the American will to continue (cost tolerance) was exceeded, and the enemy came back out to complete the job. Ultimately, those whom U.S. forces intended to save were ungrateful for their intrusion.

Peace imposition is entirely more difficult and uncertain of success than is peacekeeping. Peace imposition involves making war, especially if a peace imposer's presence is protracted (even under the guise of peacekeeping). Unless *all* the parties come to accept the peace under the conditions that the imposer creates, then it is not at all clear under what circumstances the mission can be said to be accomplished and the troops brought home. In Somalia, a version of the Aiken solution (named after the late New Hampshire senator who proposed in 1965 that the United States simply declare victory in Vietnam, without specifying what had been won, and then come home) was invoked by declaring that saving a large number of lives constituted mission accomplishment. As of late 1995, the political situation in Somalia remained chaotic.

This analysis suggests real caution about sending a large, 60,000-person force into Bosnia to monitor the peace agreement. The situation on the ground as late as November 1995 clearly indicated that not all parties were yet satisfied with the status quo. The Croatians in particular continued to be intent on grabbing back more land (especially Krajina) seized earlier by putative Bosnian Serb forces and on ethnically cleansing remaining Bosnian Serbs from those liberated zones. The Bosnian government forces were engaged in the same kind of activity on a somewhat smaller scale. All of this was coming at the expense of the gains made by the Bosnian Serbs. In those circumstances, it is hard to imagine why those benefitting from the continuation of war (at that point, the Muslims and Croats) or those wanting to recoup losses (the Bosnian Serbs) would be content with whatever status quo emerged and was enforced by the "peacekeepers." Moreover, the "federation" between Bosnian Muslims and Croatia seemed little more than a figment of the American imaginations that created it. It could fall apart in a blink of the eye, opening a whole new round of land grabbing between Muslims and Croats, possibly after IFOR leaves.

The conditions for peacekeeping, despite what the opposing parties accepted, seemed problematic. That this was not conventional peacekeeping was implied by preparations for the American participation in the beefed-up NATO-deputized force. Unlike in Somalia, the force would not be composed of lightly equipped Marines, Rangers, and the like but rather mechanized infantry and other "heavy" combat forces—in other words, the configuration of a peace-imposition force. In that case, were they to be peacekeepers, peace imposers, or that hybrid, "combat peacekeepers?" It was not clear that the distinctions had been entirely worked out.

CONCLUSIONS: U.S. POLICY TOWARD INTERVENTION

The question of whether or when to become involved in new internal wars has been a central part of the effort to redefine national-security policy and missions in the post–Cold War. The Gulf War experience led many in the policy and academic community to think in expansive terms. Within the military, figuring out how to cooperate with (rather than vilify) the United Nations became a virtual passion. In the euphoria, Somalia seemed a reasonable idea. The outcome of intervention in Somalia cooled that ardor considerably; Bosnia could be its defining standard.

The Clinton administration has taken an odyssey on this question (which I have described more fully in a chapter in Stephen Cimbala's *The Clinton Defense Policy*). It bought off on George Bush's initial intervention in Somalia, then allowed American troops to be sent back in with the widened mission of state building, apparently without sufficient understanding of the morass in which it might find itself.

During 1993 and 1994, the administration honed its policy in an effort to gauge public reaction to various stances. In September 1993, National Security Adviser Tony Lake gave the first hint, suggesting that American responses be guided by four "rules": "Is using force in America's interests? Can it [force] actually do any good? Is the cost acceptable? Is there a way out?" Taken cumulatively, the Lake rules suggest a considerable pulling back from the early apparent activism that had motivated the administration in Somalia in 1993. The list is fundamentally in harmony with the so-called Weinberger Doctrine of 1985 that sought to limit the post-Vietnam employment of American forces. General Colin Powell was present when the Weinberger Doctrine was written (some believe he actually drafted it), and he was present for the discussions that would form Clinton's policy. This was hardly a coincidence, and much of the policy's content was previewed in a 1992/93 *Foreign Affairs* article by the then chairman of the Joint Chiefs of Staff.

President Clinton laid out the basis of his policy in his September 27, 1993, speech to the UN. Beginning with the suggestion that "if the American people are to say yes to UN peacekeeping, the United Nations must learn when to say no," the President laid out a series of "threshold questions" that he believed must be asked before a peacekeeping or peace enforcement force should be considered. They closely mirror the Lake rules: "Is there a real threat to international peace and security? Does the proposed mission have a clear objective? Can an end point be identified for those who will be asked to participate? Are the forces, financing, and mandate that will be needed to accomplish the mission available?" Clinton also laid out additional criteria for *American* direct participation, a distinction that would be reflected in the final policy pronouncement.

In May 1994 the administration issued Presidential Decision Directive (PDD) 25, its ultimate policy statement. The PDD, in essence, laid out criteria for three different contingencies: support for UN peacekeeping forces when American physical participation was not included; support for UN peacekeeping efforts that do include participation; and U.S. participation in peace enforcement. The criteria are cumulative and, as might be expected, progressively restrictive.

The criteria for U.S. support of peacekeeping missions in which it does not actually participate are the least stringent. Although they are worded somewhat differently than the UN speech and Lake rules, the gist is the same. A "real threat" is one in which U.S. interests are advanced by an action, where a breach or threat to international security is involved, and where the consequences of inaction have been carefully weighed and rejected. Further, there is provision for "an understanding of where the mission fits on the spectrum between traditional peacekeeping and peace enforcement." Additionally, the mission must be tied to clear objectives and "realistic criteria for ending the operation," and appropriate funds and forces must be available.

The criteria for American troop participation expand this list. They are:

- Participation advances U.S. interests and both the unique and general risks have been weighed and are considered acceptable.
- Personnel, funds, and other resources are available.
- U.S. participation is necessary for the operation's success.
- The role of U.S. forces is tied to clear objectives and an end point for U.S. participation can be identified.
- Domestic and congressional support exists or can be marshalled.
- Command and control arrangements are acceptable.

All but the last of these requirements were included in the UN speech as well as in the Weinberger Doctrine. Acceptable command and control arrangements means command of American troops by American commanders. This anticipated the great political opposition that would have occurred domestically if the possibility of subordinating U.S. forces to foreign commanders had not been eliminated.

The criteria for involving American troops where there is the prospect of "significant U.S. participation in Chapter VII operations" that are likely to involve combat reflect Powell's penchant for overwhelming force to create quick victory with minimum casualties. The criteria are: "sufficient forces" to achieve the objectives; the existence of a plan to achieve those objectives "decisively"; and sufficient flexibility to change plans and the forces' "size, composition, and disposition" as necessary. It is not clear that the PDD recognizes the differences involved in phases one and two of counterinsurgency, as discussed in Chapter 3.

The litmus test for this policy is Bosnia, and the assessment must be mixed. When President Clinton announced his intention to participate in the NATO peacekeeping force when (or if) a stable ceasefire could be arranged, he seemed to follow his own guidelines, particularly emphasizing the necessity of American participation and command and control arrangements. The IFOR that was authorized (60,000 troops, of which 20,000 were to be American) reflects ambivalence about its use. The size of the force, as well as its composition, was clearly designed more for a peace imposition than a peacekeeping mission. The advertised reason for a large, heavily armed force was to avoid the pitfalls that befell UNPROFOR, leaving its members vulnerable and the force incapable of carrying out its mission.

As the peace process unfolded in Dayton, President Clinton remained, at least rhetorically, true to his policy guidelines. In a November 13, 1995, article in *Newsweek,* he reemphasized the criteria that would be applied before American troops would be committed to Bosnia: "I will not deploy U.S. troops to Bosnia unless the parties commit to a solid peace agreement. I will insist on NATO command and control that protects our troops and ensures the effectiveness of the operation. Our troops will take their orders from the American general who commands NATO forces—no one else. They will have clear rules of engagement, a carefully defined mission, and an exit strategy. As the peace process moves forward, I will continue to consult closely with Congress. If an agreement is reached, I will request an expression of Congressional support."

But forming a different kind of force in reaction to what happened to UNPROFOR misses the point. It was not the nature or composition of UNPROFOR that caused it to fail, but the nature of the situation. A peacekeeping force was sent to do a peace imposer's job. Now a peace imposer's force is being raised for what is supposed to be a peacekeeper's mission. The situation and the response to it have been stood on their heads, and no additional clarity has resulted from the inversion. Whether the conceptual muddle can somehow be reconciled will strongly influence assessments of the Bosnia operation and future U.S. involvement in new internal wars.

REFERENCES

Betts, Richard. "The Delusion of Impartial Intervention." *Foreign Affairs* 73, 6 (November/December 1994): 20–33.

Blodgett, Frank. "The Future of UN Peacekeeping." *Washington Quarterly* 14, 1 (Winter 1991): 30–37.

Boutros-Ghali, Boutros. *An Agenda for Peace: Preventive Diplomacy, Peacemaking, and Peace-Keeping.* New York: United Nations, 1992.

Carlsson, Ingvar. "The UN at Fifty: A Time for Reform." *Foreign Policy* 100 (Fall 1995): 3–18.

Charters, David A., ed. *Peacekeeping and the Challenge of Civil Conflict Resolution.* Fredericton, N.B.: University of New Brunswick, Center for Conflict Studies, 1994.

Clark, Jeffrey. "Debacle in Somalia." *Foreign Affairs* 72, 1 (1992/93): 109–123.

Clinton, Bill. "Why Bosnia Matters to America." *Newsweek* (November 13, 1995): 55.

The Clinton Administration's Policy on Reforming Multilateral Peace Operations. Washington, D.C.: U.S. Department of State, May 1994.

Crocker, Chester, "The Lessons of Somalia: Not Everything Went Wrong." *Foreign Affairs* 74, 3 (May/June 1995): 2–8.

Durch, William, ed. *The Evolution of UN Peacekeeping: Case Studies and Comparative Analysis.* New York: St. Martin's Press, 1993.

———. *The United Nations and Collective Security in the 21st Century.* Carlisle Barracks, Penn.: Strategic Studies Institute, 1993.

Eban, Abba. "The UN Idea Revisited." *Foreign Affairs* 74, 5 (September/October 1995): 39–55.

Gelb, Leslie. "Quelling the Teacup Wars." *Foreign Affairs* 73, 6 (November/December 1994): 2–6.

Goodman, Glenn W. Jr. "Creating a Peace to Keep." *Armed Forces Journal International,* November 1995: 18–20.

Kennedy, Paul, and Bruce Russet. "Reforming the United Nations." *Foreign Affairs* 74, 5 (September/October 1995): 56–71.

Lefever, Ernest. "Reining in the UN" *Foreign Affairs* 72, 3 (Summer 1993): 17–21.

Mendez, Ruben P. "Paying for Peace and Development." *Foreign Policy* 100 (Fall 1995): 19–32.

Powell, Colin. "U.S. Forces: Challenges Ahead." *Foreign Affairs* 71, 5 (Winter 1992/93): 32–45.

Snow, Donald M. *National Security: Defense Policy for a New International Order* (third edition). New York: St. Martin's Press, 1995.

———. "Peacekeeping, Peace Enforcement, and Clinton Defense Policy," in Cimbala, Stephen (ed.), *The Clinton Defense Program.* Westport, Conn.: Greenwood Press, 1996.

———. *Peacekeeping, Peacemaking, and Peace Enforcement: The U.S. Role in the New International Order.* Carlisle Barracks, Penn.: Strategic Studies Institute, 1993.

United Nations Peacekeeping: Update, December 1994. New York: United Nations, 1995.

6

Bloody Futures?

Analysts are just beginning to recognize the differences between the pattern of violence that evolved during the Cold War and the emerging form that typifies new internal war. In a recent *Foreign Affairs* article, Edward Luttwak calls it "post-heroic warfare" to indicate that the purposes, means, and outcomes of involvement in these wars do not conform to those of more traditional roles and missions. Throughout this book I have stressed the importance of understanding those differences before we attempt to apply solutions that were crafted for different situations. Countries of the First Tier should use great caution before becoming partners in the bloody futures that may lie ahead for many countries outside the emerging global economy and political system.

The purpose of this chapter is to summarize and extrapolate from arguments made earlier and to suggest how or whether the system, and most explicitly the United States, should become involved in staunching the bloodflow brought on by new internal war. The chapter begins with a review of how these wars are different from past internal wars and the consequences of those differences. The discussion then moves to the dynamics of intervention in these wars for the international system, including conceptual and practical problems and the reconciliation of interests and policy. I conclude by suggesting how such an analysis applies specifically to the United States and American foreign policy.

THE NEW PROBLEM OF INTERNAL WAR

The fact that new internal war is the most prominent form that violence takes in the post–Cold War world is in some ways a testimony to the general improvement of the system over the conditions in the

Cold War. Although these wars tend to be vicious in their conduct, they are fought at the periphery of the international system, not at its heart. During the Cold War, the prevention or management of conflicts in which the United States and the Soviet Union might become entangled was serious business, because the failure of deterrence could lead to the end of the international system. The new internal wars are wrenching for those involved, but they hardly create a parallel intensity of concern internationally.

The fact that these wars do not threaten the overall system in any direct way does not mean they are unworthy of consideration. They do, after all, represent the major form that violence now takes, and there is little reason to think that the pattern will change in the next few years. Occasionally one of these wars will spill over directly into the First Tier of states, as has the cause of the Algerian fundamentalists in France. Further, one of the most frequent results of the new internal war is large numbers of desperate and destitute refugees who can place a burden on the system. That burden can be direct (such as Haitian refugees headed for the United States on flimsy rafts) or indirect, in the need to underwrite governmental and nongovernmental efforts to save refugees (such as relief efforts in eastern Zaire for victims of the Rwandan rampage). This is not a trivial concern; in 1994 the UN High Commissioner on Refugees estimated there were over 19 million refugees from African conflicts alone. Moreover, if there is a disorderliness to the current system, as is so widely declared by analysts such as John Mearsheimer, these wars are its most obvious source of disorder.

Manifestations of Difference

The difference between the new internal wars and traditional insurgencies is manifested in at least five ways. The first difference is the *political dynamic* of new internal war. Traditional insurgencies are fought for the clear purpose of controlling the political system: Insurgents seek to gain control, and the government seeks to maintain its control. Appealing to the common population as a means to gain or strengthen support is a normal part of the struggle, giving insurgencies their special politico-military mix.

In a number of the new internal wars, this dynamic is not evident. In the cases of the narco-insurgencies and criminal insurgencies, there is no particular interest in gaining control of the political system in order to enact some kind of program. Instead, the objective is to maximize anarchy so that there is no authority to interrupt criminal activities. Similarly, Islamic fundamentalist movements often want to force a regime out of power because it does not adequately enforce quranic dictates, but they seldom provide structured alternatives. Neither case fits into traditional, pre-Clausewitzian categories of military culture or warrior ethic. Except when insurgents are appealing rhetorically to a high political purpose, there is no common center of gravity, no battle for the hearts and minds of the subject population. Shining Path does not seek to convert the population to its cause but merely to create terror and undermine support for the regime. The Hutu militias were not trying to convert anyone; they were trying to slaughter as many of their enemies as possible.

Although the ennobling effect of a lofty political goal affects the leadership, in terms of the kinds of actions they are likely to contemplate, authorize, and tolerate, it probably does not affect the foot soldier very much; he or she is likely motivated by boredom, atavistic dislikes for other groups, or fear of his or her leaders. I suspect that the absence of political appeal results in a higher level of cynicism throughout the ranks. In Angola, for example, where the fighting has been going on over thirty-five years, most participants report they have no idea what they are fighting for.

The lack of common centers of gravity contributes to a second difference, the generally *greater lack of restraint* in the way new internal wars are conducted. Knowing that one ultimately needs the support of the population restrains the violence of actions undertaken in traditional insurgency; not caring one way or another removes any inhibitions on what one might do. The horrible slaughter in Rwanda, the purposeful starvation of women and children in Somalia, and the random execution of uncovered women in Algeria are all acts of atrocity difficult to imagine civilized people committing. Such acts characterize a war against the internal population motivated by extreme hatred or greed.

The carnage is not unique to the contemporary scene. The exploits of the Mongol hordes of Genghis Khan in the thirteenth century would not have made very pretty television, and the earlier twentieth century has witnessed its share of atrocity as well. There was evidence of a lack of restraint during the Cold War, as in Cambodia, and the birth of the narco-insurgencies in Peru and Colombia predate the end of the Cold War (as do similar activities in Burma). What *is* notable about this combination of a political vacuum and an absence of restraint is its sheer prevalence as a proportion of internal violence. It is difficult in almost all the ongoing internal wars to discern a traditional political purpose or a traditional structure to the violence.

The third difference is that, in structure and dynamic, the new, uncivil internal wars resemble *international rather than civil wars.* Factions do not appeal to one another for support, but simply attempt to conquer, subjugate, and ultimately coerce their opponents. Their actions are not restrained by the goal of coming back together within the polity; they are instead the acts of foreign conquerors.

The fourth difference is the concentration of new internal wars in the *poorest countries, the failed states* of the system. As noted in Chapter 3, the social science literature on development from the 1950s and 1960s suggests that violence and instability is most likely to occur in those states that have entered the development process, where expectations have been raised but governments cannot or do not meet those expectations. This suggests that violence would be concentrated in states of the partially developed subtier of the Second Tier. However, the great bulk of ongoing new internal wars are instead in the poorest countries, where a combination of economic misery and government ineptitude leaves them somewhere in the range of failed, failing, or failure-prone states. In the context of a growing global economy and prosperity throughout the First Tier, and the cooperation of the First and Second Tiers in emerging regional economic associations (the Free Trade Area of the Americas and the Asia-Pacific Economic Cooperation), the isolation of states in which internal wars are occurring is even more stark.

The final difference is that the new internal wars appear *less predictable* than internal wars of the past. It is not clear whether their apparent randomness—their contribution to an apparently more chaotic international system—arises from inherent unpredictability, or from a lack of understanding on the part of First Tier governments of the phenomenon or the kinds of states in which it occurs. Although I have made some attempt to describe how these wars are carried out, I do not know of a literature that studies the dynamics that lead to a Rwandan or Somalian tragedy, for instance.

The confusion stems from a general lack of understanding of the post–Cold War system. Some elements of the post–Cold War world are obvious (the absence of a central military confrontation, the disappearance of the Soviet bloc), but the significance of the new dynamics remains unclear.

Consequences of Differences

However, there appear to be three consequences of the change from traditional to new internal war.

The first is that the new internal wars involve *higher levels of atroc-*

ity and inhumanity and that they are also less controllable from the outside. When insurgents and their opposing governments were clients of the major powers, there was some ability to constrain conduct to what sponsors found acceptable. The U.S. government, for instance, would have been terribly embarrassed had the forces it supported in Angola committed atrocities with American-provided weapons on the scale that occurred in Somalia; it would have let Jonas Savimbi and his followers know that should they engage in such acts, it would have to dump them. With the Cold War rivalry only a memory and the old sponsors removed from the scene, there is no one to provide restraint; this is particularly a problem in those states in which authoritarian regimes collapse and reveal the underlying weakness of their societies.

A second consequence is that policymakers lack an *adequate conceptual understanding* of these circumstances to be prepared to deal with them. There are two holdover conceptual frameworks that provide a potential basis for understanding, and neither is clearly applicable. The first is the model of insurgency-counterinsurgency based in some form of mobile-guerrilla warfare, as described in Chapter 3. That model is clearly applicable to traditional insurgencies in which the contending forces are competing for control of the political system and for the loyalty of the population. But it does not necessarily add to an understanding of "insurgencies" whose purpose is to destabilize the system with no intention of replacing it. The only part of the dynamic of insurgency-counterinsurgency that seems to apply is that of outside intervention. If there is a lesson from outside intervention in insurgencies, it is that it is seldom successful and almost never decisive; if the analogy holds, then it should throw some cold water on advocacies of involvement in the new internal wars. The other model, explored in more depth in Chapter 5, is that of peacekeeping. The applicability of peacekeeping language and rationales is limited to conditions of meaningful peace among former combatants. When it is applied to war zones, or to circumstances in which the parties have not given up the option of war to reach their goals, the results can be tragic.

The third consequence is the *difficulty of devising policy* toward these kinds of wars. These conflicts tend to occur in places about which fairly little is known. During the Cold War in First Tier countries intelligence efforts were concentrated on the communist world to the exclusion of those areas outside that competition—which, it turns out, is where new internal war is concentrated. If it is true, as I have asserted, that outside intervention into internal wars will always have a partisan effect, even if there is no prior partisan intent, knowing exactly what those effects might be would aid policymaking. Was there a clear idea of what effect disarming the clans in Mogadishu would have? Is Crocker tragically correct in describing the action, from the viewpoint of policymakers, the result of "mission creep"? Should it have been obvious that this creep was really a leap with quite predictable consequences? The effect of creating a safe zone for Iraqi Kurds in 1991 (Operation Provide Comfort) was an open-ended commitment for the United States, Great Britain, and France that, if abandoned, would almost certainly lead to the bloody suppression of the Kurds by the Iraqi government or the resumption of war between Iraq and the West. Was that clearly appreciated at the time? Almost certainly not.

The new internal wars almost uniformly occur outside the areas of traditional interest of First Tier powers. The exception is war that breaks out in former colonies of European states such as Great Britain or France where some residual interest may remain, but such interests hardly ever affect the United States (with the possible and limited exception of Liberia). The lack of interests makes it very difficult to sell an activist policy to a public that is the primary limitation on the use of force by First Tier countries. The rapidity with which American public opinion turned against the Somalian intervention is evidence of this problem, as was the initial lopsided public opposition to sending American troops to oversee a Bosnian peace settlement.

The Dynamics of Intervention

Understanding the dynamics and consequences of outside intervention is important to determining when, if at all, the system can and will respond. I raise four by no means exhaustive categories of potential problems associated with intervention, each of which was encountered by the United States and its principal NATO allies as they prepared for and began conducting the mission in Bosnia prescribed by the November 1995 peace agreement among the major antagonists. The first problem, which proved the major stumbling block to forming the Bosnian force in the first place, was the lack of clear and vital American interests in Bosnian peace. I have previously identified this dynamic as the interest-threat mismatch, and it is a factor that will come into play almost any time involvement in a Second Tier conflict is proposed.

The lack of compelling interests was at the heart of the partisan political debate over whether American troops should be dispatched to enforce the peace accord. No one argued that the United States was disinterested in Balkan peace; the question was *how much* interest the United States had. Opponents argued, in traditional realist terms, that vitality was missing. The Clinton administration, interestingly enough, dredged up an argument reminiscent of calls to remain steadfast in Vietnam: Because the United States had brokered the peace accord, it was a matter of both national commitment and prestige that Americans participate in the implementation of the accord. Morally, the president argued, it was "the right thing to do."

That this debate will recur in the future is almost inevitable and flows from the American status as the remaining superpower in the post–Cold War era. Arranging for a peace agreement among the Serbs, Croats, and Muslims was a stunning (if highly reversible) accomplishment, but coming as it did on the heels of similar efforts among Israel and its neighbors (including the Palestinians), it established an expectation for the United States as peacemaker that will be difficult to shed. The structure of the political argument, however, will remain the same. The relevance or "fit" of the realist-dealist paradigm may have disappeared with the end of the Cold War.

The second problem was to define the nature of the war and hence the problems that had to be reconstructed. The nature of the war in Bosnia was thoroughly unmilitary: as there was very little combat among the supposed armies of the three sides. Rather, military and paramilitary units mostly terrorized the civilian populations of the other groups to convince them to leave their homes so as to facilitate annexation to one preferred entity or the other. Residual problems included assigning responsibility for the many atrocities committed, and the massive relocation of refugees (estimated at 2 million) from the war. Although the military nature of the Bosnian situation was peculiar in the parties' fascination with annexing maximum amounts of territory, its unmilitary nature is hardly unusual at all. The "wars" in central Africa, and the narco-insurgencies, are also largely of this nature.

The political nature of the war is a concern as well. The delicate territorial boundaries of the Bosnian-Croat and Serbian autonomous regions required large-scale population transfer, and the workability of the complex constitutional system seemed uncertain, particularly given the widespread distrust created by the war itself. On the surface, the arrangement seemed to incorporate elements of the old, failed Yugoslav system (the rotating presidency, for instance). At the same time, war-crimes trials vexed an already strained situation.

The third major problem was how to conceptualize the force that would be sent into Bosnia. As training began, there was no clear consensus. Military spokesmen pointed out that this would not be a traditional peacekeeping force, for which the size (60,000 troops) and heavy armament would have been inappropriate. At the same time, there was a loud protestation that this also would not be a peace imposition force, because the force would not be deployed until there was a peace agreement and a discernible peace on the ground. As a result IFOR was conceptualized as a sort of hybrid—more robust than a peacekeeping force but not a force to create a peace and hence leap the divide from peacekeeper to state builder.

Early apologists used the peace-enforcement label to describe the mission. Apparently this was not intended to follow the classic Boutros-Ghali formulation of recreating a breached peace (although such was not ruled out) but to follow the literal meaning of the term: enforcing a peace in existence. This formulation, however, left at least three unanswered questions. The first was of what exactly the hybrid consisted. It was not passive peacekeeping or aggressive peace imposition; yet there remains much operational and conceptual space between those extremes. This led to a second question: If the role was not peace imposition, why was the United States sending such heavy forces (the First Mechanized Infantry Division) to the scene? Such troops are configured and trained for offensive, aggressive combat, not for overseeing the separation of former combatants. Their assignment was, in all likelihood, seen primarily as a hedge against encountering the humiliations of the underarmed UNPROFOR troops, as a way to minimize the number of American casualties, and as a way to intimidate the civilian population so that it would not interfere with the mission. Whether that configuration was best suited to this hybrid exercise is something time will resolve.

The third question pertains to the analogy between this kind of mission and intervention as counterinsurgent. Given the spotted history of outside intervention, Rod Paschall, for instance, argues that it "is not an enterprise in which the West should risk the prestige of its armed forces," especially when the military itself regards "peacekeeping as a secondary and unwelcome duty." In the relative absence of alternative duties, peacekeeping/peace enforcement/peace imposition may seem attractive; if it is as ultimately difficult and frustrating as intervention in counterinsurgency, the bloom may soon be off the rose.

A greater effort is needed to define exactly what kinds of situations (new internal wars) the United States and the rest of the First Tier may face, how their dynamics differ from those of traditional internal wars, and exactly what kinds of forces and missions will be involved. The early discussions about IFOR suggest the need for greater conceptual refinement.

The fourth problem, a derivative of the counterinsurgency analogy, was how the IFOR forces were to remain neutral in any continuing disagreement among the parties. Due to the hybrid nature of the agreement, and the self-proclaimed role of United States as honest broker of the peace process, it was clear that the mission would be effective only as long as it remained strictly impartial—a primary requisite of true peacekeepers, as will be recalled from Chapter 5. This necessity seemed inconsistent with the announcement that part of the mission of American forces would be to train and equip the Bosnians as the time for pulling out of Bosnia approached.

This raises the collateral dynamic, so evident in Vietnam and Somalia, that the actions of the IFOR forces would be unappreciated by the native population, especially if their role became, or was perceived to have become, partisan. When calls for a NATO presence were first raised as early as 1992 and 1993, it was fairly clear that a peace-imposition force inserted into Bosnia would effectively be allied to the Bosnian Muslims (who were losing at the time). To the extent that any side seeks to alter the status quo on the ground and is thwarted by IFOR, the perception of partiality is almost inevitable.

The decision to become involved in Bosnia is potentially a watershed event for the United States in its involvement in new internal war. Exploring those implications will be the purpose of the concluding section of this chapter. To do this it is necessary to explore some of the consequences of the problems identified above, as well as some remaining conceptual and practical problems of intervention.

CONSEQUENCES AND PROBLEMS OF INTERVENTION

The dynamics of intervention suggest that such actions should be taken with considerable caution, given that the likelihood of success is not high. This implication is reinforced by an examination of the consequences of those dynamics. The consequences can be grouped into four categories: the problem of military conceptualization; the political definition and problems of intervention; public reluctance to support these kinds of enterprises; and international consequences of intervention or inaction. These problems refer to situations involving peace imposition or peace enforcement—the active or potential use of force—rather than traditional peacekeeping. There are two reasons for this. The first is that peacekeeping situations are minimally stressful and incorporate few of the dynamics of uncivil war discussed in Chapter 5. The second is that traditional peacekeeping rarely directly affects American policy or forces, other than possible token logistical or physical participation.

Military Problems

The problem of military conceptualization is the most important because the greatest distortions and misunderstandings of the dynamics of intervention occur at the military level. The basic problem is an underestimation of the difficulty—even futility—of substantially improving internal-war situations. The problem originates in the conceptualization of possible military operations within the framework of peacekeeping. That conceptualization is wrongheaded in that it tends to make the action seem simpler than it is, and that it tends to avoid or ignore the root problems of state building.

Peace imposition has almost all of the characteristics of intervention in a counterinsurgency. Indeed, the closest correlation between traditional insurgency-counterinsurgency and new internal war is found at this level. Starting from that perspective clarifies the problem and, because no truly effective strategy for intervention in insurgencies has evolved, strongly suggests caution in approaching potential involvements in peace-imposition operations.

There are three consequences of starting from this military perspective. The first is that any potential operation must recognize the two stages of counterinsurgency. The first stage consists of avoiding defeat and involves the use of heavy, massed forces against insurgents operating in the third stage of mobile-guerrilla warfare. By analogy, the insertion of large, sophisticated forces (as were used in Bosnia and, to a lesser degree in Haiti) serves the purpose of intimidating the contestants and causing them to cease hostilities for fear of antagonizing the interveners. The problem with successful completion of the first stage is that it predisposes the intervenor (and those whom the intervention was intended to aid) to believe that more of the same is called for. In the process, the objective of the second stage, pacification and winning the support of the population, may be subordinated. Because popular acceptance of the imposed peace is the ultimate goal of the enterprise, the failure to consider both stages of counterinsurgency can doom the mission to long-term failure.

The second consequence is closely related to the first. Internal wars are both military and political phenomena, in which suppression of the violence alleviates the symptom of the malaise but can rarely effect its cure: the political process of reconciliation or state building. For example, the underlying problem in Bosnia, for which IFOR could be no more than a shield, was the reconciliation of peoples torn apart by history and four years of very unmilitary warfare. The third consequence, drawn from the Vietnam War experience, is that outsiders cannot build a stable state for the natives. Outside intervention may be necessary when the internal contestants prove incapable of ending the fighting themselves, but can those outsiders change the internal conditions in the country so that the violence will not recur? In the Bosnian situation, the Americans were able to press the warring parties to accept a peace plan, and the NATO force sent into the country could reasonably keep the sides from one another's throats for the period of its mandate. Ultimately, however, reconciliation in Bosnia has to be an act of the Bosnians themselves.

Political Problems

The second set of problems results from the political definitions involved in intervention. Most fundamentally, the political definition must begin from the realization that lasting solutions in most of these situations involve some form of state building. Generally speaking, they occur in states in one of the stages of failure discussed in Chapter 4, which means that the problems are fundamental and difficult to solve. Moreover, an intervenor must recognize that solutions, where they are possible, will be slow, expensive, and arduous. The analogy with intervention in counterinsurgencies continues to hold in the sense that the intervenor has to recognize the very real limits on its ability to influence outcomes and the fact that the level of its involvement is inversely related to the likelihood of success.

A related political reality is the likely ingratitude that some or all members of the host country will come to display toward the peace imposers. The implicit peacekeeping analogy, which begins from the premise of neutrality, acts perversely here. Peacekeepers can maintain neutrality and the gratitude of the population because they enter peace zones and, more fundamentally, do not attempt to change the political or military balance. Peace imposers, by contrast, will *always* alter that balance by stopping fighting that some or all parties prefer to continue.

This ingratitude has a second aspect. For peace imposers to ensure that the political processes of state building or restoration have a firm start requires a relatively long-term commitment. This will increase the unease of public opinion in the imposer's country, especially if ingratitude is expressed violently, and will likely prompt charges of neocolonialism within the host country that will increase opposition to the mission. The United States avoided this problem in Haiti by limiting the length of its stay; whether IFOR will have similar luck will be a major part of its legacy.

The third problem is public reluctance to become involved in these kinds of missions. When such missions are considered, they will normally occur in places and over situations in which important U.S. interests, traditionally defined, are not clearly at stake. Part of the overall problem is convincing the American public that the proposed action warrants support. Sometimes this can be temporarily finessed: The sight of starving Somali children overwhelmed hard-headed initial debate. At other times, important interests can, in effect, be invented: President Clinton declared that U.S. prestige would be irreparably compromised if it did not contribute to a Bosnian peace.

Because traditional interests are rarely going to be at stake in these situations, however, public support is always likely to be fragile and volatile. There will always be some patina of philanthropy, and if those subject to the philanthropy do not respond with appropriate fealty, the support base will erode (particularly if ingratitude results in the remains of American soldiers being returned in body bags). Long, open-ended commitments will inevitably witness an erosion of public support as well. This is vitally important to recognize because real solutions require deeper commitments. There is the possibility that public opinion can condemn the peace imposers to treating symptoms but never solving underlying causes, a practice that will prove eventually unsatisfying.

The fourth problem involves the international consequences of intervention, and it has at least three aspects. The first is the question of the legitimacy of involvement in internal wars. International law is very clear on this matter: Except for limited incursions for the purpose of rescuing a country's own nationals from war zones (as the United States did in Liberia in 1996), intervention is illegal even at the request of one of the parties. The problem was particularly difficult in Somalia, which essentially had no government to either invite or condemn the invasion it received. Passing UN Security Council resolutions does not add to the legal weight of an intervention, although many seem to believe that it does.

The second aspect is the precedential nature of intervention. Intervention in an internal war, regardless of the purity of motive that underlies it, is a direct violation of territorial sovereignty. Sovereignty is the cornerstone of the modern state system and is, presumably, not a principle to be violated capriciously. One may argue on humanitarian grounds that there is a "superior" right to protect humanity against acts of atrocity and even genocide. That argument may have a lofty ring to it, but it promotes an alternative basis of organizing and legitimizing the operation of the international system. At what point does the accumulation of interventions constitute a precedent for changing the international law of sovereign jurisdiction?

This question is by no means an easy one, because honoring traditional notions of sovereignty suggests an international-system reaction of inaction. The failure of the system to respond to acts of genocide (and most of the so-called humanitarian interventions are at least partially justified under the UN Convention on Genocide) is also precedential. The international system may not want to send the message that anything goes as long as it remains within the territorial jurisdiction of a single state.

The third aspect flows from the savagery with which so many of the new internal wars are conducted. Many of these are hardly wars at all, because the "combat" consists primarily of one or more sides terrorizing and savaging innocent civilians rather than engaging each another militarily. The result in Rwanda and Bosnia was to reactivate war crimes statutes and to attempt to bring war-criminals to justice. There are likely to be more instances for which war-crimes charges will be appropriate, and the precedent set with the tribunals for Rwanda and Bosnia could send strong messages to those who would engage in future rampages against civilian populations. This will be particularly true in the Bosnian case due to the much higher public profile that NATO's monitoring of the process has created internationally, and to the fact that both the president and the leading general of the Bosnian Serbs have been indicted.

CONCLUSIONS: THE IMPLICATIONS FOR U.S. POLICY

The U.S. decision to spearhead the Implementation Force in Bosnia illustrates the policy quandary that faces the United States in the more general context of new internal war. The Bosnian case demonstrated clearly the centrality of American leadership in any systemic reaction to a large internal problem. This is the price of being the world's remaining superpower; the price of brokering the Bosnian peace agreement was the promise of prominent American military participation. As President Clinton put it in his November 27, 1995, speech to the American people, "People all around the world are now looking to America for leadership. So let us lead." At the same time, the speech acknowledged that involvement in "securing" the peace in Bosnia did not represent a blanket endorsement for activism around the world. "We cannot stop all war for all time but we can stop some wars," Clinton said.

The rationale for entering Bosnia asserted that peace and stability are basic American interests, and sought to expand the area of vitality by arguing that, because the United States put the deal together, its prestige would be vitally injured if it did not act. The issue of whether Balkan peace and stability (assuming that is obtainable at all) represents an important American interest deeply divided the population at the time the decision was made, and will almost certainly resurface if the mission does not ultimately succeed. Putting American prestige on the line, and then declaring the need to protect it, is a circular proposition that could be used to justify actions where few if any traditionally defined American interests are at stake. Ultimately, the success or failure of IFOR will clarify the definition of interests worth putting the lives of American service persons at risk. This will help build the new framework for dealing with violence in the post–Cold War world.

The experience in Bosnia will also go a long way toward assessing the merit of my argument for caution in intervening in internal wars. I have argued that these wars are dissimilar to traditional insurgencies because of the absence of any shared center of gravity to modify the violence and serve as the core for reconciliation after the war is over. Moreover, these wars often occur in states at some point in the process of failure; the ultimate solution requires state building and considerable economic development, neither easy to do. Bosnia certainly qualifies as a situation in which there is no battle for the hearts and minds of men, which will make reconciliation more difficult. State building will be less of a problem, although intergroup representation and the Muslim-Croat alliance will probably take years to sort out. Presumably, Europe will open its checkbook to deal with the economic dimension. In these senses, the problem of Bosnia is "easier" than those of Sierre Leone and Somalia, where the tasks of state building and economy building are daunting.

My argument for caution has a military basis as well, stemming from the analogy between intervention in insurgencies and involvement in internal wars. The analogy is clearest in peace-imposition situations, wherein the wretched record of intervention in insurgencies during the Cold War may well be replicated by similar experiences in post–Cold War internal wars. How has American policy stood up to these challenges? The Clinton administration has been widely accused of vacillation, and the president has been criticized for his lack of military service (and hence his lack of empathy for the military). These criticisms seem politically motivated and, I would assert, they miss the point. Current circumstances are sufficiently different from the problems encountered during the Cold War that policymakers are moving through uncharted waters. If there has been vacillation (and there has been), it is the result of groping in the dark for answers.

In the political dimension, the United States has made progress in devising criteria for involvement in different forms of intervention. These criteria—for voting for and supporting UN actions, American participation in peacekeeping, and American participation in peace imposition—are conservative and increasingly strict as more active and dangerous involvement is envisaged. They closely reflect both the Weinberger doctrine and the Powell doctrine of decisive intervention.

In his rationale for U.S. participation in IFOR the president was careful to adhere to those criteria. He did not (probably because he could not) specify which of the three situations Bosnia represented. By stating the goal as "helping the people of Bosnia to secure their own peace agreement," he implied that IFOR was more than a standard peacekeeping force in the UN sense. But because there was a peace agreement, it was not exactly a peace-imposition force either. Rather, the heavily equipped forces sent to Bosnia represented a hybrid; their mere presence was supposed to intimidate those who preferred the continuation of war. If peace begins to break down, the forces are ready to stop the fighting ("peace enforcement," in the UN sense). Given the nature and armament of the forces, they are prepared to deal with a fairly large failure, a situation requiring something close to peace imposition. It was not clear at the time of the pronouncement whether the mandate from the American people extended to the latter mission, which would amount to war.

The military dimension appears somewhat more problematic. Although it was said at the time IFOR was being formed that the military had learned enough from past missteps, notably in Vietnam and Somalia, to be ready for the Bosnian mission, it is not clear that this was the case. The American military lacks experience in these kinds of actions, and thus it has no strategy for handling them. The choice of troops sent into Bosnia displays a lack of understanding of the difference between peacekeeping and peace enforcement/imposition missions. Mechanized infantry, the backbone of the force, is an offensive combat force whose specialty is confronting and defeating similarly armed forces. Whether they can adapt to a role that may be no more than peacekeeping without degrading their fighting skills is questionable. The attitude expressed privately within the upper echelons of the military that any good soldier can be a peacekeeper is only a hypothesis, and one of dubious merit.

Beyond Bosnia

Going beyond the Bosnian case to the more generalized question of involvement in new internal war, there are at least three policy implications for the U.S. government that are worth exploring. The first is for an expanded and improved intelligence capability for dealing with these situations. The bulk of them will occur in Africa, the southern rim of the old Soviet Union, and South and Southeast Asia. None of these are areas of great traditional expertise within the American government. The military and civilian intelligence agencies have long been staffed by analysts with expertise in the former communist world; almost half the analysts with the Directorate of Intelligence of the Central Intelligence Agency have their primary expertise in the former Soviet Union and Eastern Europe. Within the armed services, a prime source is the Army's Foreign Area Officers (FAO) program, but that has always been something of a "career buster" for those who enter it.

Better knowledge of the situations within countries experiencing new internal wars is necessary for both political and military purposes. Political judgment about the desirability or feasibility of involvement at any level is necessary to prevent these wars or to assess what, if anything, can be done about them. Could superior intelligence have averted the Rwandan rampage? How much did the United States know about the political balance in Somalia on the eve of American involvement? Officials such as Robert S. McNamara are just beginning to admit that the United States knew too little about Vietnamese nationalism when it decided to intervene there. Can we afford to continue in such ignorance?

The deep connection between military and political actions in insurgency and outside intervention suggests more military sophistication as well. It is characteristic of irregular warfare (and even if the new wars do not meet historic standards of irregularity, they certainly *are* irregular) that it is difficult to discern friend and foe. In Vietnam the failure to do so led to everyone being considered the enemy, resulting in attacks against innocent civilians with disastrous political repercussions. The military target in internal war makes a great difference in whether missions succeed; better information must be available to forces on the ground in these matters.

The second policy implication is the need for greater interagency cooperation when mounting involvements in new internal wars. The strong political dimension of these wars suggests a need for cooperation between the State Department (which will generally have the lead position except in peace imposition/enforcement situations), the Defense Department (including the individual services), and the intelligence community. There is considerable lip service to this end, but real implementation is a more difficult matter. Moreover, the need for cooperation goes beyond traditional relations within the government, extending at least to nongovernmental organizations on the ground in humanitarian or observer roles. NGOs are generally present when forces arrive, and they are important for providing basic services in war zones. The enormous logistical system of the U.S. armed forces suggests that more formalized cooperation in what the military calls "humanitarian relief operations" could alleviate a great deal of human suffering in these circumstances. The airlifting of machinery to provide potable drinking water, sanitary facilities, and medicine to the Rwandan refugee camps in Zaire may be a prototype for such action in the future. Since the NGOs are there when missions arrive and remain after the forces leave, it makes sense to devise a viable "hand-off" strategy to maximize cooperation between American forces and relief agencies, and to maximize the likelihood that the NGOs will be left with the best possible situation when the forces are withdrawn.

The need for cooperation extends to a third policy area, the need for international cooperation. One reason to involve the United Nations early in the post–Cold War world was to engage in "burden sharing," spreading responsibility for actions as widely as possible so that the United States (or anyone else) does not bear a disproportionate amount of the burden. Framing the IFOR response within the framework of NATO was a similar attempt to apportion the responsibilities. Given American reluctance to become involved in these kinds of actions, the perception that the United States is doing more than its fair share would almost certainly doom future involvement.

This list is doubtless incomplete, but then, so is our understanding of new internal war. Although it is difficult to devise scenarios in which these kinds of conflicts could convulse the system at large, it is certain that they will persist and possibly increase in frequency and severity. What we do know about the new internal wars suggests that involvement in them should be approached with extreme caution. But because they are likely to remain the major source of violence and instability in the system for the foreseeable future, they cannot be ignored altogether.

REFERENCES

"Clinton's Words on Mission to Bosnia: 'The Right Thing to Do.'" *New York Times* (national edition), November 28, 1995: A6.

Killebrew, Robert B. (Col., USA). "Combat Peacekeeping: Fashioning an American Approach to Intervention Operations." *Armed Forces Journal International,* October 1995: 34–35.

Luttwak, Edward N. "Toward Post-Heroic Warfare." *Foreign Affairs* 74, 3 (May/June 1995): 109–122.

McNamara, Robert S. *In Retrospect: The Tragedy and Lessons of Vietnam.* New York: Times Books, 1995.

Mearsheimer, John J. "Why We Shall Soon Miss the Cold War." *Atlantic Monthly* 266, 2 (August 1990): 35–50.

Paschall, Rod. *LIC 2010: Special Operations and Unconventional Warfare in the Next Century.* Washington, D.C.: Brassey's (U.S.), 1990.

Appendix
Second Tier, by Region and Subtier

ASIA AND PACIFIC

Developed

Hong Kong
South Korea
Singapore
Taiwan

Partially Developed

China
India
Indonesia
Malaysia
Micronesia
Marshall Islands
North Korea
Thailand
Vanuatu

Developable

Afghanistan
Bangladesh
Bhutan
Burma (Myanmar)
Cambodia
Fiji
Kiribati

Laos
Maldives
Nepal
Pakistan
Papua New Guinea
Philippines
Solomon Islands
Sri Lanka
Tonga
Vietnam

Resource Rich

Brunei

MIDDLE EAST

Developed

Cyprus
Israel

Partially Developed

Egypt
Lebanon
Malta
Oman
Syria
Turkey

Developable

Jordan
Yemen

Resource Rich

Bahrain
Iran
Iraq

Kuwait
Qatar
Saudi Arabia
United Arab Emirates

LATIN AMERICA

Developed

Argentina
Brazil
Chile
Mexico
Venezuela

Partially Developed

Antigua
Bahamas
Barbados
Belize
Bolivia
Colombia
Costa Rica
Dominica
Ecuador
Grenada
Guatemala
Jamaica
Panama
Paraguay
St. Kitts-Nevis
St. Lucia
St. Vincent
Suriname
Uruguay

Developable

Cuba
Dominican Republic
El Salvador

Guyana
Haiti
Honduras
Nicaragua
Peru

Resource Rich

Trindad and Tobago

FORMERLY COMMUNIST COUNTRIES

Developed

Slovenia

Partially Developed

Croatia
Czech Republic
Hungary
Kazakhstan
Poland
Russia
Slovakia
Ukraine

Developable

Albania
Armenia
Azerbaijan
Belorus
Bosnia and Herzegovina
Bulgaria
Estonia
Georgia
Kyrgyzstan
Latvia
Lithuania

Macedonia
Moldova
Mongolia
Romania
Tajikistan
Turkmenistan
Uzbekistan
Yugoslavia (Serbia and Montenegro)

Resource Rich (0)

AFRICA

Developed

South Africa

Partially Developed

Angola
Botswana
Cameroon
Congo
Djibouti
Ivory Coast
Mauritius
Morocco
Nigeria
Zimbabwe

Developable

Benin
Burkina
Burundi
Cape Verde
Central African Republic
Chad
Comoros
Equatorial Guinea

Eritrea
Ethiopia
Gambia
Ghana
Guinea
Guinea-Bissau
Kenya
Lesotho
Liberia
Madagascar
Malawi
Mali
Mauritania
Mozambique
Namibia
Niger
Rwanda
São-Tomé and Príncipe
Sierre Leone
Senegal
Seychelles
Somalia
Sudan
Swaziland
Tanzania
Uganda
Zaire
Zambia

Comprehensive Bibliography

Allison, Graham, and Gregory Treverton, eds. *Rethinking America's Security: Beyond Cold War to New World Order.* New York: W. W. Norton, 1992.

Altschiller, Donald. *The United Nations' Role in World Affairs.* New York: H. H. Wilson, 1993.

Bacevich, A. J. et al. *American Military Policy in Small Wars: The Case of El Salvador.* Cambridge, Mass.: Institute for Foreign Policy Analysis, 1989.

Bell-Fialkoff, Andrew, "A Brief History of Ethnic Cleansing." *Foreign Affairs* 72, 3 (Summer 1993): 110–121.

Betts, Richard. "The Delusion of Impartial Intervention." *Foreign Affairs* 73, 6 (November/December 1994): 20–33.

Bissell, Richard E. "Who Killed the Third World?" *Washington Quarterly* 13, 3 (Fall 1990): 23–32.

Blank, Stephen J. and Earl H. Tilford Jr. *Russia's Invasion of Chechnya: A Preliminary Assessment.* Carlisle Barracks, Penn.: Strategic Studies Institute, 1995.

Blodgett, Frank. "The Future of UN Peacekeeeping." *Washington Quarterly* 14, 1 (Winter 1991): 30–37.

Bloomfield, Lincoln. "The Premature Burial of Global Law and Order: Looking Beyond the Three Cases from Hell." *Washington Quarterly* 17, 3 (Summer 1994): 145–162.

Boutros-Ghali, Boutros. *An Agenda for Peace: Preventive Diplomacy, Peacemaking, and Peace-Keeping.* New York: United Nations, 1992.

———. "Empowering the United Nations." *Foreign Affairs* 72, 5 (Winter 1992/93): 89–102.

Brodie, Bernard. *War and Politics.* New York: Macmillan, 1973.

Brown, Harold. *Thinking About National Security: Defense and Foreign Policy in a Dangerous World.* Boulder, Colo.: Westview Press, 1983.

Brown, Seyom. *New Forces, Old Forces and the Future of World Politics: Post–Cold War Edition.* New York: HarperCollins, 1995.

Bueno de Mesquita, Bruce. *The War Trap.* New Haven, Conn.: Yale University Press, 1981.

Burk, James, ed. *The Military in New Times: Adapting Armed Forces to a Turbulent World.* Boulder, Colo.: Westview Press, 1994.

Carllson, Ingvar. "The UN at Fifty: A Time for Reform." *Foreign Policy* 100 (Fall 1995): 3–18.

Carothers, Thomas. "Democracy and Human Rights: Policy Allies or Enemies?" *Washington Quarterly* 17, 3 (Summer 1994): 109–117.

Charters, David A., ed. *Peacekeeping and the Challenge of Civil Conflict Resolution.* Fredericton, N.B.: University of New Brunswick, Center for Conflict Studies, 1994.

Clark, Jeffrey. "Debacle in Somalia." *Foreign Affairs* 72, 1 (1992/93): 109–123.

Clausewitz, Carl von. *On War.* Princeton, N.J.: Princeton University Press, 1976.

Clinton, Bill. "Why Bosnia Matters to America." *Newsweek* (November 13, 1995): 55.

The Clinton Administration's Policy on Reforming Multilateral Peace Operations. Washington, D.C.: U.S. Department of State, May 1994.

"Clinton's Words on Mission to Bosnia: The Right Thing to Do." *New York Times* (national edition), November 28, 1995: A6.

Crocker, Chester. "The Lessons of Somalia: Not Everything Went Wrong." *Foreign Affairs* 74, 3 (May/June 1995): 2–8.

Damrosch, Lori Fisler, ed. *Enforcing Restraint: Collective Intervention in Internal Conflicts.* New York: Council on Foreign Relations Press, 1993.

Davies, James, ed. *When Men Revolt and Why.* New York: Free Press, 1976.

DeBray, Regis. *Revolution in the Revolution? Armed Struggle and Political Struggle in Latin America.* New York: Monthly Review Press, 1967.

Diehl, Paul. *International Peacekeeping.* Baltimore, Md.: Johns Hopkins University Press, 1993.

Doder, Dasko. "Yugoslavia: New War, Old Hatreds." *Foreign Policy* 91 (Summer 1993): 3–23.

Doll, William J., and Steven Metz. *The Army and Multinational Peace Operations: Problems and Solutions.* Carlisle Barracks, Penn.: Strategic Studies Institute, 1993.

Durch, William, ed. *The Evolution of UN Peacekeeping: Case Studies and Comparative Analysis.* New York: St. Martin's Press, 1993.

———. *The United Nations and Collective Security in the 21st Century.* Carlisle Barracks, Penn.: Strategic Studies Institute, 1993.

Eban, Abba. "The UN Idea Revisited." *Foreign Affairs* 74, 5 (September/October 1995): 39–55.

Etzioni, Amatai. "The Evils of Self-Determination." *Foreign Policy* 89 (Winter 1992/93): 21–35.

Flint, Julie. "On the Wrong Side of a Jihad." *World Press Review,* November 1995: 37–38 (reprinted from *The Independent* of London).

Friedman, Thomas L. "The Next Rwanda." *New York Times* (national edition), January 24, 1996: A15.

Fukuyama, Francis. "The End of History?" *National Interest* 16 (Summer 1989): 3–18.

———. *The End of History and the Last Man.* New York: Free Press, 1992.

Gati, Charles. "From Sarajevo to Sarajevo." *Foreign Affairs* 71, 4 (Fall 1992): 64–78.

Gelb, Leslie. "Quelling the Teacup War." *Foreign Affairs* 73, 6 (November/December 1994): 2–6.

Giap, Vo Nguyen. *People's War, People's Army.* New York: Praeger, 1962.

Goodman, Glenn W. Jr. "Creating a Peace to Keep." *Armed Forces Journal International* (November 1995): 18–20.

Gorbachev, Mikhail S. *Perestroika: New Thinking for Our Country and the World.* New York: Harper and Row, 1987.

Gotlieb, Gidon. *Nation Against State: A New Approach to Ethnic Conflicts and the Decline of Sovereignty.* New York: Council on Foreign Relations Press, 1993.

Greentree, Todd. *The United States and the Politics of Conflict in the Developing World.* Washington, D.C.: U.S. State Department Center for the Study of Foreign Affairs, 1990.

Guevara, Ernesto ("Che"). *Guerrilla Warfare.* New York: Monthly Review Press, 1961.

Gurr, Ted Robert. *Minorities at Risk: A Global View of Ethnopolitical Conflicts.* Washington, D.C.: United States Institute for Peace Press, 1993.

———. "Peoples Against States: Ethnopolitical Conflict and the Changing World System." *International Studies Quarterly* 38, 3 (September 1994): 347–378.

———. *Why Men Rebel.* Princeton, N.J.: Princeton University Press, 1973.

Gurr, Ted Robert, and Barbara Harff. *Ethnic Conflict in World Politics.* Boulder, Colo.: Westview Press, 1994.

Haass, Richard N. *Intervention: The Use of American Military Force in the Post–Cold War World.* Washington, D.C.: Carnegie Endowment Books, 1994.

———. "Military Force: A User's Guide." *Foreign Policy* 96 (Fall 1994): 21–36.

Helman, Gerald B., and Steven R. Ratner. "Saving Failed States." *Foreign Policy* 89 (Winter 1992/93): 3–20.

Hilsman, Roger. *American Guerrilla: My War Behind Japanese Lines.* Washington, D.C.: Brassey's (U.S.), 1990.

Howard, Michael. *The Causes of War.* Cambridge, Mass.: Harvard University Press, 1983.

Huntington, Samuel P. "Clash of Civilizations." *Foreign Affairs* 72, 3 (Summer 1993): 22–49.

———, *The Third Wave: Democratization in the Late Twentieth Century.* Norman, Okla: University of Oklahoma Press, 1991.

Janowitz, Morris. *The Military in the Political Development of the New Nations.* Chicago, Ill.: University of Chicago Press, 1964.

Job, Cvijeto. "Yugoslavia's Ethnic Furies." *Foreign Policy* 92 (Fall 1993): 52–74.

Kampelman, Max M. "Secession and the Right of Self-Determination: An Urgent Need to Harmonize Principle with Pragmatism." *Washington Quarterly* 16, 3 (Summer 1993): 5–12.

Keegan, John. *A History of Warfare.* London: Hutchison, 1993.

Kegley, Charles W. Jr., and Gregory A. Raymond. *A Multipolar Peace? Great Power Politics in the Twenty-First Century.* New York: St. Martin's Press, 1994.

Kennedy, Paul, and Bruce Russet. "Reforming the United Nations." *Foreign Affairs* 74, 5 (September/October 1995): 56–71.

Killebrew, Robert B. (Col. USA). "Combat Peacekeeping: Fashioning an American Approach to Intervention Operations." *Armed Forces Journal International,* October 1995, 34–35.

Kober, Stanley. "Revolutions Gone Bad." *Foreign Policy* 91 (Summer 1993): 63–84.

Krauthammer, Charles. "The Unipolar Moment." *Foreign Affairs* 70, 1 (1990/91): 23–33.

Layne, Christopher, and Benjamin Schwartz. "American Hegemony—Without an Enemy." *Foreign Policy* 92 (Fall 1993): 5–23.

Lefever, Ernest. "Reining in the UN" *Foreign Affairs* 72, 3 (Summer 1993): 17–21.

Luttwak, Edward N. "Toward Post-Heroic Warfare." *Foreign Affairs* 74, 3 (May/June 1995): 109–122.
Mahnken, Thomas G. "America's Next War." *Washington Quarterly* 16, 3 (Summer 1993): 171–188.
Manwaring, Max G., ed. *Uncomfortable Wars: Toward a Paradigm of Low-Intensity Conflict.* Boulder, Colo.: Westview Press, 1991.
Mao tse-Tung. *The Collected Works of Mao tse-Tung.* Beijing: Foreign Language Press, 1957.
Marcella, Gabriel. *Haiti Strategy: Control, Legitimacy, Sovereignty, Rule of Law, Handoffs, and Exits.* Carlisle Barracks, Penn.: Strategic Studies Institute, 1994.
Mazarr, Michael J. *The Revolution in Military Affairs: A Framework for Defense Planning.* Carlisle Barracks, Penn.: Strategic Studies Institute, 1994.
McNamara, Robert S. *In Retrospect: The Tragedy and Lessons of Vietnam.* New York: Times Books, 1995.
Mearsheimer, John J. "Why We Shall Soon Miss the Cold War." *Atlantic Monthly* 266, 2 (August 1990): 35–50.
Mendez, Ruben P. "Paying the Price of Development." *Foreign Policy* 100 (Fall 1995): 19–32.
Metz, Steven. *America in the Third World: The Future of Counterinsurgency.* Carlisle Barracks, Penn.: Strategic Studies Institute, 1995.
———. *Counterinsurgency: Strategy and the Phoenix of American Capability.* Carlisle Barracks, Penn.: Strategic Studies Institute, 1995.
———. *The Future of the United Nations: Implications for Peace Operations.* Carlisle Barracks, Penn.: Strategic Studies Institute, 1993.
Metz, Steven, and James Keivit, *The Revolution in Military Affairs and Conflicts Short of War.* Carlisle Barracks, Penn.: Strategic Studies Institute, 1994.
Moynihan, Daniel Patrick. *Pandaemonium: Ethnicity in World Politics.* New York: Oxford University Press, 1993.
Mueller, John. *Quiet Cataclysm: Reflections on the Recent Transformation of World Politics.* New York: HarperCollins, 1995.
Natsios, Andrew S. "Food Through Force: Humanitarian Intervention and U.S. Policy." *Washington Quarterly* 17, 1 (Winter 1994): 129–144.
Nye, Joseph S. Jr. "The Changing Nature of World Power." *Political Science Quarterly* 105, 2 (Summer 1990): 177–192.
———. "Peering into the Future." *Foreign Affairs* 73, 4 (July/August 1994): 82–93.
O'Neill, Bard. *Insurgency and Terrorism: Inside Modern Revolutionary Warfare.* Washington, D.C.: Brassey's (U.S.), 1990.
Orwell, George. *Burmese Days: A Novel.* London: Secker and Wartburg, 1986.
Papp, Daniel S. *Soviet Policies Toward the Developing Countries During the 1980s: The Dilemmas of Power and Presence.* Maxwell AFB, Ala.: Air University Press, 1986.
Paschall, Rod. *LIC 2010: Special Operations and Unconventional Warfare in the Next Century.* Washington, D.C.: Brassey's (U.S.), 1990.
Pfaff, William. "Invitation to War." *Foreign Affairs* 72, 3 (Summer 1993): 97–109.
———. *The Wrath of Nations: Civilization and the Furies of Nationalism.* New York: Simon and Schuster, 1993.
Pickering, Thomas R. "The UN Contribution to Future International Security." *Naval War College Review* 46, 1 (Winter 1993): 94–104.

Powell, Colin. "U.S. Forces: Challenges Ahead." *Foreign Affairs* 71, 5 (Winter 1992/93): 32–45.

Project Plowshares. *Armed Conflicts Report: Causes, Conflicting Parties, Negotiations, 1993.* Waterloo, Ont.: Institute of Peace and Conflict Studies, 1994.

Rostow, W. W. *The United States in the World Arena.* New York: Harper and Row, 1960.

Rice, Edward E. *Wars of the Third Kind: Conflict in the Underdeveloped Countries.* Berkeley, Calif.: University of California Press, 1988.

Rothgeb, John M. Jr. *Defining Power: Influence and Force in the Contemporary International System.* New York: St. Martin's Press, 1993.

Sarkesian, Sam. *America's Forgotten Wars: The Counterrevolutionary Past and Lessons for the Future.* Westport, Conn.: Greenwood Press, 1984.

Schultz, Donald E., and Gabriel Marcella. *Reconciling the Irreconcilable: The Troubled Outlook for U.S. Policy Toward Haiti.* Carlisle Barracks, Penn.: Strategic Studies Institute, 1994.

Shafer, D. Michael. *Deadly Paradigms: The Failure of U.S. Counterinsurgent Policy.* Princeton, N.J.: Princeton University Press, 1988.

———. "The Unlearned Lessons of Counterinsurgency." *Political Science Quarterly* 103, 1 (Spring 1988): 57–80.

Shultz, Richard H. Jr. "Low Intensity Conflict: Future Challenges and Lessons from the Reagan Years." *Survival* 32, 4 (July/August 1989): 359–375.

Singer, Max, and Aaron Wildavsky. *The Real World Order: Zones of Peace, Zones of Turmoil.* Chatham, N.J.: Chatham House, 1993.

Smith, Tony. "Making the World Safe for Democracy." *Washington Quarterly* 16, 4 (Autumn 1993): 197–218.

Smith, W. Y. "U.S. National Security After the Cold War." *Washington Quarterly* 15, 4 (Autumn 1992): 21–34.

Snow, Donald M. *Distant Thunder: Third World Conflict and the New International Order.* New York: St. Martin's Press, 1993.

———. *National Security: Defense Policy for a New International Order* (third edition). New York: St. Martin's Press, 1995.

———. "Peacekeeping, Peace Enforcement and Clinton Defense Policy," in Cimbala, Stephen (ed.), *The Clinton Defense Program.* Westport, Conn.: Greenwood Press, 1996.

———. *Peacekeeping, Peacemaking, and Peace Enforcement: The U.S. Role in the New International Order.* Carlisle Barracks, Penn.: Strategic Studies Institute, 1993.

———. *The Shape of the Future: The Post–Cold War World* (second edition). Armonk, N.Y.: M. E. Sharpe, 1995.

Snow, Donald M., and Eugene Brown. *The Contours of Power: An Introduction to Contemporary International Relations.* New York: St. Martin's Press, 1996.

Snow, Donald M., and Dennis M. Drew. *From Lexington to Desert Storm: War and Politics in the American Experience.* Armonk, N.Y.: M. E. Sharpe, 1994.

Stofft, William A., and Gary L. Guertner. *Ethnic Conflict: Implications for the Army of the Future.* Carlisle Barracks, Penn.: Strategic Studies Institute, 1994.

Sullivan, Gordon R., and James M. Dubik. *War in the Information Age.* Carlisle Barracks, Penn.: Strategic Studies Institute, 1994.

Sullivan, John D. "Democracy and Global Economic Growth." *Washington Quarterly* 15, 2 (Spring 1992): 175–186.

Summers, Harry Jr. *On Strategy: A Critical Analysis of the Vietnam War.* Novato, Calif.: Praesidium Press, 1982.

Sun Tzu. *The Art of War.* Translated by Samuel P. Griffith. Oxford, U.K.: Oxford University Press, 1963.

Thompson, Loren B., ed. *Low-Intensity Conflict: The Pattern of Warfare in the Modern World.* Lexington, Mass.: Lexington Books, 1988.

Thompson, Sir Robert. *Make for the Hills: Memoirs of the Far Eastern Wars.* London: Lee Cooper, 1989.

Tilford, Earl H. Jr. *The Revolution in Military Affairs: Prospects and Cautions.* Carlisle Barracks, Penn.: Strategic Studies Institute, 1995.

United Nations. *United Nations Peace-Keeping: Update, December 1994.* New York: United Nations, 1995.

U.S. Army. *Guide to the Study of Insurgency.* Ft. Huachuca, Ariz., 1989.

Weiss, Thomas G. "Intervention: Whither the United Nations?" *Washington Quarterly* 17, 1 (Winter 1994): 109–128.

———. "New Challenges for UN Military Operations: Implementing an Agenda for Peace." *Washington Quarterly* 16, 1 (Winter 1993): 51–66.

Zakaria, Fareed. "A Conversation with Lee Kuan Yew." *Foreign Affairs* 73, 2 (March/April 1994): 109–126.

Index

About the Book

Don Snow points out that the new internal wars tend to occur in the least developed countries, the so-called failed states. He argues that, compared with participants in the internal wars of the Cold War era, these new combatants are more likely to narrow their appeal to a specific ethnic group. They are less restrained in their use of brutality and terror—and less inclined to seek broader popular and international support for their causes. Their ideological or political objectives are often vague; they may be less interested in the installation of a new government than in the profit they derive from continuing instability and lawlessness.

Snow examines how changes in the international system have encouraged the development of the new internal wars, the dominant form of conflict in the post–Cold War world. He considers how the wars may affect the security of the larger global system, as well as the role that the United States, other countries, and international organizations may have in moderating their occurrence.

Donald M. Snow is professor of political science at the University of Alabama. He has also taught at the U.S. Army War College. His previous publications include *Distant Thunder: Third World Conflict and the New International Order; The Shape of the Future;* and three editions of *National Security.* He is coauthor, with Eugene Brown, of *Puzzle Palaces and Foggy Bottom: U.S. Foreign and Defense Policymaking in the 1990s* and *The Contours of Power: An Introduction to Contemporary International Relations.*